Writing Better Fundraising Applications

A practical guide with worked examples, exercises and ideas for worksheets

Writing Better Fundraising Applications

A practical guide with worked examples, exercises and ideas for worksheets

Michael Norton
Mike Eastwood

2nd Edition

With contributions from
Liam Black, The Big Issue in the North
and John Naylor, The Carnegie United Kingdom Trust

DIRECTORY OF SOCIAL CHANGE

In association with the
Institute of Charity Fundraising Managers

Published by
The Directory of Social Change
24 Stephenson Way
London NW1 2DP
Tel: 0171 209 5151, fax: 0171 209 5049
e-mail: info@d-s-c.demon.co.uk
from whom further copies and a full publications list are available.

The Directory of Social Change is Registered Charity no. 800517

First published 1992
Second edition 1997

ISBN 1 900360 20 9

British Library Cataloguing in Publication Data
A catalogue record for this book is available from the British Library

Cover design by Kate Bass
Designed and typeset by Linda Parker
Printed and bound by Biddles, Guildford, Surrey

Directory of Social Change London Office:
Courses and Conferences tel: 0171 209 4949
Charityfair tel: 0171 209 1015
Research tel: 0171 209 4422
Finance and Administration tel: 0171 209 0902

Directory of Social Change Northern Office:
3rd Floor, Federation House, Hope Street, Liverpool L1 9BW
Courses and Conferences tel: 0151 708 0117
Research tel: 0151 708 0136

Contents

About the book

This is a practical guide on how to write a good fundraising application. The book covers much more than the actual writing of an application. It shows you what information you will need to have available before you put pen to paper, and how to get it. Good fundraising isn't simply about bashing out a few letters to possible funders. You need to build your credibility, develop grant-winning ideas and construct a realistic budget which will not leave you short of money at the end of the day. This book looks at all of that. It also suggests some things to do with your application once you have sent it off.

Writing applications is an art, not a science. There is no 'identikit' good application. What works well for one organisation may not work for another. So if your current efforts are bringing you the desired results, there is no need to change your style or approach to match the advice given in this book. But there are some general lessons which are well worth learning, and it will almost always be possible for anyone to write a better fundraising application.

You should also note that a good application will not in itself lead to success in fundraising. Donors want to know that you are a successful organisation, able to spend your money cost-effectively on a good project. It is your work they are paying for, not a nicely written and prettily presented proposal. But a good application is one part – and an important part – of a successful fundraising approach.

Occasionally, and this is particularly the case with grants from statutory sources and the National Lottery, you will need to complete an application form. However, all the same principles apply as for writing an application. You simply have less freedom as you are restricted to the requirements of the application form.

Finally, don't give up easily. Just because you are turned down once does not automatically mean that the application was poor, or the project is unfundable. Learn any lessons you can, but keep at it. Even the best fundraiser doesn't get money every time. If they did, the life of a fundraiser wouldn't be as interesting!

Michael Norton
Mike Eastwood

1 Introduction: What Makes a Good Application

Fundraising is selling a good idea

Fundraising is all about selling an idea to someone who has the means to make it happen. If you are successful, you will get the money, sponsorship, support in kind or commercial service that you need. You have to make the donor interested in your ideas. And if they are interested enough, then they will want to help you by giving support.

There are many ways of asking. You can ask directly in person. You might make a presentation at a meeting or to a group of potential supporters. You may use the telephone (a key and vastly under-rated fundraising aid). Or you might send a written proposal. In practice, the more direct and the more personal your approach, the more likely you are to be successful.

In fact, one successful fundraiser for a homelessness project recently commented that whenever he had persuaded the potential funder to visit him at the project, he had never failed to get money from them. They saw the homeless people and the work the project was doing, and the donation followed very quickly.

This book is about writing a better proposal. But the advice is equally relevant to anyone considering any other form of approach.

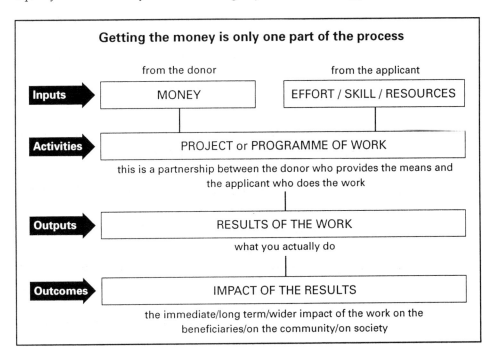

Getting the money is only one part of the process

	from the donor	from the applicant
Inputs	MONEY	EFFORT / SKILL / RESOURCES

Activities ▶ PROJECT or PROGRAMME OF WORK

this is a partnership between the donor who provides the means and the applicant who does the work

Outputs ▶ RESULTS OF THE WORK

what you actually do

Outcomes ▶ IMPACT OF THE RESULTS

the immediate/long term/wider impact of the work on the beneficiaries/on the community/on society

The importance of making a good case

There are many ingredients in a successful fundraising approach: a good project, the credibility of your organisation, the individuals involved in the work, and the interest of the person being approached will all be crucial. But it is important to remember that the approach itself is an opportunity for you to make a good case, state your need and ask for support.

A good proposal may not get a bad project funded. But a poor proposal might considerably reduce your chances of success. It is important to put forward the best possible case when you have the opportunity to do so. People fail to do this surprisingly frequently – as some of the worked examples in Chapter 8 show.

By improving your proposal you will improve your fundraising effectiveness. You are more likely to raise the money your organisation needs – and you will do this with greater confidence, with less effort and at lower cost.

The key steps in drawing up a proposal

You may set out your proposal in a brief letter, or as a weighty document describing the project in great detail. You may produce a printed brochure to send out with a brief covering letter as part of a major appeal campaign, or you may send a direct mail approach to thousands of potential supporters.

However you plan to produce your proposal, the following are the steps you will need to take:

- develop your project idea into a form which will attract support;
- identify possible sources of funds for the project. You will also need to find out as much as you can about the interests and concerns of the funder;
- understand WHY that particular funder might be interested in supporting your work. This is more than simply stating WHAT you plan to do;
- outline a plan for the long-term funding arrangements of the project (if you expect it to carry on after the initial funding elapses);
- write your ideas down as a proposal for support clearly, coherently, forcefully and enthusiastically;
- identify the best person to make the approach. This will be the person who will sign the letter and be involved in any telephone follow-up and subsequent meetings;
- decide how and when to make the approach. An immediate

Ten steps to success in fundraising

---

1. **Keep the facts at your fingertips**
   Make sure that all the information you will need about your organisation and about the project is readily available. Back up your argument with facts and figures; don't just make assertions.

2. **Build your credibility**
   Get yourself and your organisation known in the grants world, develop effective public relations, get (good) publicity for your work. Don't underestimate the value of just meeting donors informally and chatting. This is often when the best fundraising is done.

3. **Develop grant-winning ideas**
   Some ideas and projects are so good that they have no difficulty in being funded. Think about your work and see if there are ideas or projects which will more easily win a grant.

4. **Sort out your fundraising strategy**
   Think about how your organisation is to be funded over the next few years, whether this is realistic and what you need to do to put your organisation's funding on a secure basis. Think about how you intend to attract funds for the project immediately and on a continuing basis (if the project is to continue).

5. **Research and identify likely grant prospects**
   Avoid the scatter-gun approach. Make carefully targeted approaches at a few funders rather than writing a circular letter to anybody and everybody. Cross-reference your ideas and projects with likely funders, matching their interests to your needs. Also, be sure you know which budget the money is coming from. For example, if you are approaching a company, you could be looking for support from the donations budget, corporate PR, marketing or personnel department, or even its staff relations committees. Your approach would need to be adapted accordingly.

6. **Write a good proposal**
   Write a clear and succinct application, making a really good case for support.

7. **Manage the application process**
   Decide how and who is to contact the funding source, whether a formal proposal should be put to them right away, whether a meeting or visit could usefully be arranged, and how you can bring more influence to bear on the decision-making process. Also, should you be the person making the approach? Would it be better if it came from someone else? (A colleague might have more established contacts with the funders, or a prestigious trustee or supporter may have more impact.)

8. **Say 'thank you'**
   If you succeed in getting a grant, note any restrictions or obligations on your part and make sure you comply with these. Say 'thank you' immediately.

9. **Keep in touch**
   Maintain contact with those who are supporting you (obviously), but also with those who are not (where you feel they are or should be interested in your work). Report on your successes and continue to build your credibility with them.

10. **Go back**
    Ask those who have supported you for further support next year or the year after – they have already demonstrated that they like you and what you are doing. Go back to those who have turned you down – if you feel that they should be interested. Persistence really can pay. Note any reasons given for rejection. It may be worth finding out whether there is a chance of reapplying and trying to fix up a meeting to discuss your proposals further.

approach may not work out best. You may wish to make preliminary contact or enter into informal discussions first, before you submit a formal proposal. The funder may also have particular requirements for the submission of applications which you need to know;

■ make the request, indicating as specifically as you can **how** and **how much** the funder might contribute.

The function and purpose of the proposal

When making a proposal to a funder, you will be aiming to:

1. Raise money (or other support) for your organisation and its work. This obviously is your number one objective

2. Raise as much money as you can from the particular funder you are approaching. You will need to know what level of support the donor is likely to give and whether you can expect and obtain a regular grant rather than just a one-off payment. If you do not raise the maximum amount from each funder, this is a missed opportunity and will increase the amount of fundraising work you will have to do.

3. Promote your organisation and its work. Whether or not you are successful, the funder will know more about you as a result of the approach. So even if you are not successful this time, you may have laid the groundwork for a successful approach in the future.

Applications basics

People often try to write an application as a means of working out what they should be doing. This is a recipe for disaster. Preparation is the key. The more you get ready in advance, the easier and quicker you will find it to write a good proposal. Thinking, planning, discussing, budgeting, re-thinking, re-planning and re-budgeting all take time, but it is time well spent. You need to get together the following information **before** you send off the application.

1. Your selling points

A few key reasons why the work you are doing is important and why donors will want to support you. Remember, there is a massive difference between saying what you are doing and stressing why it is important and worth supporting.

2. Facts and figures about your work

Research, statistics or figures which will help demonstrate the importance of your cause, the extent of the need, the value of your work and the success of the methods you are using to carry out the project.

3. The credibility of your organisation

Endorsements and statements from other people which enhance the importance of your work and what you are trying to achieve. They should give the donor increased confidence in your ability to deliver the work you are promising to do.

4. A plan and budget for your project

You need to be clear what you intend to do, how and when you intend to do it, and what the benefits will be. These can be written up into a simple project plan. You can then put together a financial plan for what you propose, properly and fully costed and covering all the items of expenditure you plan to incur. It should also include any income you expect to generate from the project.

5. Donor research

Find out what the funder is interested in and the scale of support you might expect if your application succeeds (i.e. what to ask for), and identify any connections between you and the funder (personal contacts, previous approaches for support).

6. Back-up literature

Have brochures, annual reports, quotes sheets and other good information available to attach to your written proposal. These will enhance your case and improve your chances of success.

Now you are ready to start writing your application.
Advice and ideas on all these points are given in the following chapters.

The ingredients of a successful application

- *Your key selling points*
- *Facts and figures*
- *Credibility and endorsements*
- *Project plan and budget*
- *Donor research*
- *Back-up literature*
- **A well-argued case**

---

2 The Ingredients of a Good Application

Your key selling points

Most major funders receive thousands of applications each year. Yours has to catch their attention and stand out of the pile as something worth supporting.

You need to do more than tell them what you plan to do. You have to tell them why your work is important and why it makes sense for them to support you.

You will need to make a number of key points which catch the reader's attention, arouse interest and 'sell' the proposal.

For example, what is unique, special and different about the work you are doing? Why is it necessary and important? What will it achieve? What will grab the interest or excitement of a funder? Why would they want to give you the money to do it?

You have limited space to get these points across, and you need to use the space effectively. Deciding the key points to make will help you do this.

Here are some of the points you might consider making.

You should try to tell people why your work is important, not just what you do.

1. The problem and the need

Voluntary organisations exist to meet important needs (e.g. elderly people being isolated and neglected; young people at risk of crime or abuse; disabled people being discriminated against; the environment being destroyed by overuse and pollution).

Organisations must believe in what they do, enthuse about their achievements and the income they have raised. If you can't be clear and enthusiastic about the work you are doing, a potential funder certainly won't be. You must define the problem in words they can understand and in a way that makes them feel they want to do something about it. If you can't show why it is really important that your work develops, you will not get the money.

Try not to generalise. Many applications simply make bland assertions such as 'we work with young people excluded from school' or 'everybody knows that we have a serious drugs problem amongst young people and the problem is growing'. You need to do much more than this. You need to show the following:

- **What is the nature of the problem you are tackling?**
  For example, 'More and more young people are developing long-term health problems through lack of exercise'.

- **How widespread is it?**
  You need evidence for your claims. For example, 'Over 50% of children aged 11–16 watch more than three hours of television each night. Only 5% regularly do more than four hours physical exercise each week'.

- **Why is it important?**
  Don't assume that the reader understands the problems you are describing. Spell it out to them. Stress the importance of what you are doing and why something must be done now. If you can't, the funder may prefer to turn to someone else who can. For example, 'Already health specialists are warning that this level of inactivity at an early age is storing up serious heart problems for the future. Indeed, as a leading cardiologist recently said: ...'.

- **What are the consequences of the problem or need, and what will happen if nothing is done?**
  Show how the situation will get worse and worse as the problem grows more acute. For example, 'The surgical costs alone are expected to double to over £x million a year. This does not take account of the economic costs of increased absence from work owing to ill health'.

- **Are there any social trends which demonstrate that the problem will increase in the next few years?**
  Prevention is usually cheaper than cure; it is certainly preferable. So, if you can show how changes in society are likely to make the situation worse, these will add weight to your argument. For example, 'If people do not develop the capacity to take exercise early in life, they can effectively be cutting out a whole series of leisure options later on. As people retire earlier this could have a serious impact on their quality of life in retirement because ...'.

- **What kind of people will be helped as a result of your work, and why are their needs particularly important?**
  If you have not made it clear already, describe clearly who will benefit and in what way are they disadvantaged (e.g. through poverty, ill health, disability, lack of facilities).

■ Exercise: Ask yourself the following questions

1. What are the needs of our users?
(If you're not getting anywhere, try to describe the difficulties a typical user may be having to face.)

2. What will happen to them if we don't do anything?

3. Can we prove this?

4. What will happen to them if we do something?

5. Can we prove this?

If you are a local project, you will also need to answer the following question:

■ **What are the particular features of your area or community that make it specially important to give you support?**
Not all communities are the same. Why is the need great in your area (e.g. no-one else is doing anything, you have a high percentage of young people excluded from school, or whatever)?

Try to answer all these questions. Be as specific as you can. Give facts and figures wherever possible. Do not make generalisations or use hollow phrases such as 'urgent problem' or 'desperate need'. One or two key statistics can do more for your case than a page of well-intentioned waffle.

Also, and crucially, all the above is about the people you are trying to help, not about the needs of your organisation. So many people apply because 'we need a minibus' or 'we need a new building'. Why? At this stage, don't talk about your own needs, stress the needs of your intended users or beneficiaries. Show what difference you (and the funders) can make to their lives.

2. Your proposal

It is not enough to convince the funder that there is a real and urgent need to be met; you also need to show them that you have a sensible and practical solution to the problem. Again, you should be enthusiastic. Try to excite the donor by showing that something positive and effective can be done. Some ways of doing this are listed below.

■ State clearly what you are going to do
Don't just say: 'We will work with the relevant agencies to encourage young people to become more active at an early age'. How are you

going to do this? You need to be specific. For example – and continuing with the health risk example above – you could say: 'We will develop a series of basic training programmes that any young person will be able to follow. It will only require 15 minutes exercise, three days a week. Many can be done alongside existing day-to-day activities'.

- **How can you guarantee that it will work?**
  You can't! However, you can show what practical steps you will be taking to ensure that there is every chance of success. So: 'Local celebrities – including X Olympic champion – will visit every school and youth club in the area to talk to children about the health risks they run without proper physical exercise. They will hand out the basic training programmes and do a demonstration exercise with the children. They will follow this up with repeat visits to the schools and clubs. We will also run activity sessions in school holidays in which …'.

- **How will you measure success?**
  Many grant-makers are moving towards 'output' funding, where they gauge the success of the project on the measurable things it achieves. What targets are you going to set for the project? Or, as the National Lottery Charities Board puts it, 'list up to three ways your project will make a difference and tell us when these results are likely to happen. Please describe how you will measure and record these results'.

Again, to use the above example: 'Our project will visit each school in the area three times a year; we will visit each youth club at least once a year. This means we will speak to W thousand children and hand out X thousand training programmes. Based on our previous pilot study, we expect Y hundred to attend at least one of our school holiday activity sessions. And anybody who successfully completes level 8 of the programme will get a certificate personally signed by ***. We aim to present Z hundred of these certificates at schools and youth clubs each year.'

Try to give the funder a clear plan of action, including numbers involved, where, when and how it will all happen.

3. Your effectiveness and cost-effectiveness

- **Can you demonstrate that your work is effective?**
  Have you got a good track record? Have you gone from strength to strength? Or at least, have you done one thing really well? Can you show that you have achieved real results before? If so, what were they and why were they so great? Can you get a supportive quote from someone that the funder will respect? In fundraising terms, success breeds success.

- **Can you show that what you plan to do is an efficient and cost-effective way of dealing with the problem?**
  How many people will be helped? How many will use the facilities? And at what cost per person and with what results? Ideally, you should be able to show high numbers at low cost. For example, 'The schools pack will only cost £5,000 to produce but will be used by over 20,000 young people over the next three years'.

- **What will be the outcome of your work?**
  Outcomes are what happens as a result of your work – not just what you do, but the impact it has and the changes that take place. For example, in an employment training project, it is not just the number of people trained that is important but the number of people who get proper employment as a result, and the number that continue in employment after a year.

- **Does your work represent value for money and does it compare well (or better) to alternative approaches to dealing with the problem?**
  Showing value for money is an increasingly important part of your fundraising, especially to trusts and the National Lottery Charities Board. They want to make sure that they are getting the maximum benefits from the money they spend.

You could show how much money you will be saving. For example, drug-related crime costs £X per week and you may get, on average, five people a year off drugs. This saves £Y amount. Alternatively, you may stop people turning to crime; you may prevent environmental decay; you may stop people staying away from school; you may prevent people having to have expensive medical treatment. You should be able to put a cash value on all of these savings.

On the other hand, can you show that you generate money? You may get people into employment; your advice sessions may result in Y hundred people receiving £X thousand in unclaimed benefits; you may help people save money on heating bills; you may be able to develop a service that you can charge for which will underpin your organisation's financial security. Again, you are showing how a small amount of money now leads to a long-term benefit well in excess of the value of the grant given.

Knowing the effectiveness, the impact and the cost-effectiveness of your work can help you make a good case. It can also help you manage your project better. Monitoring and evaluation are an important aspect of your work. If you can show success, people will want to support you.

Not everything has to be done at the lowest cost. You need to balance the quality and quantity of your output. If you are dealing with special needs which require particular effort, or if you are doing more than just papering over the problem, then this too can be a point in your favour. Show how you are getting to the heart of the problem that everyone else is ignoring while the cost of the neglect just grows and grows. However, if you appear 'expensive', make sure you explain why this is still the lowest realistic cost for meeting this really important need.

4. Other plus points

There are a whole range of other key points that you may wish to make.

- **Your use of volunteers.** Time is precious. If people willingly give you some of theirs you must have something in your favour. You may also give volunteers transferable skills and training opportunities.

- **The involvement of users and ex-users in running the programme.** They may be part of the problem, but they can often be part of the solution.

- **The involvement of users in the drawing up and planning** of the project or in the management of the organisation. Show that you don't know best and that you are not trying to impose your ideas, but that the plans and ideas have come from those who really know – the users.

- **Your ability to mobilise support in kind.** Show that you can think around a problem, that you are not just cash-obsessed.

- **Your ability to attract support from other sources**, and particularly from the statutory sector.

- **Your financial security** and **sustainability** in the medium and long-term. Show that you are a safe bet.

- **The proportion of funds you generate** or propose to generate yourselves. Self-help at every level is very attractive to funders.

- **The support you get in membership or donations** from the local community. Having community support is another strong plus point.

- **Collaboration with other organisations**. Show how you avoid unnecessary duplication and overlap, and that you thereby provide a comprehensive service.

- **Leverage** – that is being able to demonstrate a large impact produced from a relatively small amount of support, or how the grant will be used to mobilise further support.

All these will be seen as plus points by funders. They will show you as resourceful and effective, and show funders that their pounds will be well 'invested' with you, creating, as the Americans say, 'more bang for the buck'.

You must be able to come up with several good reasons why your project should be supported. You need to make these the key 'selling points' in your proposal. You may well not be able to get all of them into every application. Rather, highlight those of specific interest to that particular donor.

It is a good idea to work out what your key selling points are, and then to discuss and agree them with your colleagues and your management committee or trustees. These points will be the basis on which you present your organisation when you are seeking support, so it is important that they reflect how people within the organisation see the organisation and its work.

If there is anything you are unhappy with or any point where you feel that the organisation could do better, this is something that should be addressed as a management issue by the organisation. Anyone trying to raise money for an organisation must believe that it is doing the best job it can and, if there are problem areas – as there often are – that the organisation is doing its best to sort these out.

Understanding your weaknesses

'Imagine the following situation: a church member comes to you and says she'd like to open a crèche for working mothers. She's put together a rota of willing volunteers to staff it and there is an obvious need for such a service within the congregation. It will pay for itself and the rooms she wants are not required for any other purpose. Could you come up with half a dozen reasons why it's totally impractical? If so, you could be just the person we're looking for to be our next CHURCH WARDEN.'
(From *A Survivors' Guide to the Church*)

Selling points: an example

A local youth club will highlight different selling points when appealing to different donors. Here are some points you might make:

1. To the local authority

- You are running a service which is 'professional', using qualified leaders and meeting all the technical and other requirements. Previous club members are now trained leaders.
- You are efficient – you attract the correct ratio of young people to session leaders or staff.
- You are effective and are known to run an excellent service.
- There is a need – your catchment area has a high incidence of need and a low provision compared with other areas.
- You are cost-effective and provide value for money.

2. To the parents of local young people

- You provide a 'containment service', keeping young people off the streets and out of harm's way.
- You provide an educational service – your programme of activities is attractive and beneficial and young people acquire new skills and interests.
- You take young people to places they otherwise would not be able to get to, or they undertake activities they have never done before.
- You do all this at extremely low cost – only a few pounds per term.

3. To grant-making trusts

- There is a real need and you are unique – as before.
- Your work is well thought of and you have achieved maximum possible funding from statutory sources.
- The project you are proposing is an interesting development or an innovative approach to dealing with a certain problem. If successful, other groups could copy it.
- You are using new media (e.g. arts, sport or information technology) to engage with young people and that particular trust has an interest in that medium.
- Other trusts have supported and are supporting you.

4. To local companies

- You are keeping your people off the streets and from doing harm. You might even give an implication that the funders have a vested interest; if they help, the level of vandalism (including that of their property) will be reduced!
- There are educational, training, work experience benefits, all concerns of interest to companies. Ultimately you can offer them high quality recruits.
- You are a well-run and successful local charity, which it makes sense for them to support out of a sense of local community responsibility.
- Children of company staff are/have been youth club members and/or current leaders are company employees.
- The company will get good publicity in the local press in return for the grant – and you can show evidence that you have obtained such publicity before.

■ Your selling points: an exercise

Try to write down at least three selling points under each of the following headings. Ask other people in the organisation what they would say too.

We meet the following need(s)...

The needs we meet are particularly important because...

The following shows that we are effective...

We are different/unique because...

Our other strengths are...

If we did not exist then...

Funders usually prefer to support successes rather than failures. Therefore, you need to be able to show a track record of successes. List your five greatest successes in recent years (e.g. in the past five years).

1.

2.

3.

4.

5.

If you get stuck, complete the following sentence:

We are the best because...

A common reaction by someone reading your proposal is to think up all the reasons why they should reject it. Some typical reasons might be:

'There are too many charities already doing the same thing, and we are already funding *** charity.'

'I've never been to... (somewhere in the sticks – or the North!)... and I don't see why we should be spending our money there.'

'I've never heard of them so they can't be doing a very good job.'

'They have run up a huge deficit. I don't see why we should continue to pour money into them.'

'They spend far too much on administration.'

'They are extremely rich; they have enormous assets and reserves. So they don't need our help.'

'They are an expensive service. I think we could spend our money more wisely elsewhere.'

'I remember the bad publicity when two members of their management committee resigned.'

'Their work is extremely controversial.'

'They are too political' (meaning they campaign a lot or are too left wing).

You need to be aware of the potential problems or difficulties people may raise about your organisation. Different donors will be concerned about different things. For example, a company may be looking for a clean image, whereas a grant-making trust will want to know that they are not paying for a lost local authority grant. You need to get inside the minds of the donors and address their concerns accordingly.

When you look at your organisation and its weaknesses, there may well be a perfectly good explanation for most of the apparent problems. You then have to decide whether to confront the issue head on, by mentioning the 'problem' and the explanation in your proposal, or whether just to be prepared with a satisfactory answer if you are ever asked questions about it. It is not very sensible simply to forget that the 'problem' exists.

Often, your fundraising is by letter and supporting materials. There is usually no meeting and no opportunity to discuss things in more detail at a later stage. Therefore, it is usually best to try and neutralise any of the possible objections within the letter. This requires careful writing. You do not want to be as clumsy as to say: 'you [the funder] might be thinking 'gosh this is really expensive'. Let me show you how is isn't.' Rather, you explain that the cost of dealing with the problem is X. This is much more cost-effective than the conventional Y approach, and is certainly much cheaper than the Z cost of not doing anything at all. Or, if you have been running a deficit and therefore appear financially weak and generally badly managed, show how this year you will break even and next year you will even move into surplus. You could explain, for example, that the deficits were a necessary outcome of important structural changes you made, that the organisation is now much stronger and how the project you are writing about is central to the organisation's on-going development and financial viability.

Sometimes, you may have to delay your application until you have resolved some of your problems. Or at least you may have to bring them to the attention of your management committee and get them to sanction certain courses of action. You can then show the funder how you are already on the road to sorting the problem out.

With the National Lottery Charities Board (NLCB) you need to be particularly aware of your apparent failure to meet their assessment criteria. For example, they take equal opportunities and user involvement very seriously. If you cannot show user involvement in your work – and especially the project you are trying to get money for – you will reduce your chances of success. Therefore, you will need to adopt strategies to demonstrate that although you have been historically weak in the area of user involvement, you are now taking the issue very seriously. You can then show how all future projects, especially those funded by the NLCB, will match their desired criteria. At least with the NLCB you have the assessment stage to make these points, but part of the NLCB applications game is pre-guessing where they will mark you down, and showing them that by the time this new project gets going you will be well on the way to meeting their concerns.

Getting and using facts and figures

It will always be helpful to be able to illustrate the strength of your case by using facts and figures rather than making generalised statements such as 'there is a desperate need' or 'the problem has increased dramatically in recent years'. It is far better to show exactly how great the need is or how fast the problem has been increasing. Indeed, many funders now require hard information rather than your opinions or perceptions.

Facts and figures should be objective. Try not to allow the prejudiced funder to think 'Well, they would say that, wouldn't they?'. Get information from impartial sources which have no vested interest in seeing your project succeed, and use this to make your case for you.

A couple of choice facts can be far more effective than two paragraphs of argument. For example, a survey in an area of North West England showed that women who have been physically abused

Dealing with weaknesses

An example

Say you have lost money in each of the last three years. The funder may look at your accounts and think that you are slowly but surely going under and you will not be able to undertake the work you have asked them to fund. Obviously you need to reassure them that this isn't the case. How can you do this?

■ **Explain why the losses came about**

For example, are they the result of a major relocation or re-structuring (financial or staff)? If so, you can show how you have reached the end of this process and are now moving forward. Or are they the result of losing a major grant or income stream? If so, show what steps you have taken to address the short-term problem of replacing the funding (or making the necessary financial savings), and that you have put or are putting in place a new, secure and more wide-ranging income base.

■ **Show how you are progressing well this year**

Hopefully this year things are going better. Can you show that you have budgeted for a financial surplus and that you are on target to meet this? This implies that things genuinely have begun to turn around.

■ **Use a business plan**

Draw up a business plan (if you haven't done so already) which shows how you expect to make a regular surplus over the next 3 – 5 years, again pointing out the significant changes you have made and will be making to enable you to achieve this.

■ **Indicate the funder's role in your development**

It may be that you are applying to the funder specifically to help you get out of the financial mess you are in. Again, you will need to give them the confidence that you have thought through your long-term income and expenditure requirements and that you have a workable strategy in place to achieve this. Then show the funder the importance of your work and that they can be a key investor in your organisation's future growth and development.

Make a list of some of your weak points and how you might respond.

Weakness	*Explanation*

by their partners had to go, on average, to eight different agencies before they could get meaningful help. In two lines you have demonstrated an absolute and irrefutable need for a better system.

Don't assume that the facts and figures will speak for themselves. You may need to explain what the statistics mean, why your area is higher than the national average, why there is a growth in the level of need, why the changes are important, and so on.

Facts and figures are obtainable from a variety of sources:
- **Local and central government reports and surveys**, local health authority reports, reports of parliamentary Select Committees, the National Audit Office etc.
- **Official government statistics** such as Census data, Population Trends, Social Trends, Regional Trends and the General Household Survey.
- **A variety of other publications** including reports by special interest groups and campaigns (e.g. The Joseph Rowntree Foundation, Child Poverty Action Group, Cancer Research Campaign, King's Fund).
- **Your own researches** (e.g. questionnaires to your users, clients, potential users, local community).
- **Academic research** published in journals and books.

Building credibility

Fundraising is as much who you know (and who knows you) as what you do. Indeed, it is sometimes said that fundraising is 10% what you know and 90% who you know. The figures may not be that extreme, but it is important to know and be known. Organisationally you need to be known, liked and trusted. It also helps if you are personally known, liked and trusted.

Many professional grant-makers will have heard of you well before you have even discovered them. It is their business to know what is happening and to identify the successful projects and organisations that are making things happen. However, don't just wait for them to find you. It is your business to get yourself noticed and to establish a reputation of being a successful organisation which is doing good work. Funders support you because they believe in you and your organisation's ability to run good projects, as much as in the specific project for which you are seeking funds.

Assume that a funder agrees that you have demonstrated a clear and important need and that you have a sensible plan to deal with the problem. Their next question is: 'That's all very well, but how can I trust this lot to deliver on this?' This question will partly be answered by how good and clear your solutions to the problem are. However, you also need to establish your credibility.

Sometimes funders will support you because they have heard about your work and believe in it, sometimes because they have come into contact with you, sometimes because of a personal contact or commendation, sometimes because they have heard of the patrons, trustees or prominent people associated with your cause. All of these can be as important as the quality of work you are doing and the excellence of your written proposal.

You need to show:

Your ability and professionalism

Show that you are a well-run outfit, that you have grown over the years, that you are soundly financed, that you have a wide support base, that you have a range of qualified staff, that you run a comprehensive volunteer training programme or whatever. The days of the enthusiastic amateur are by no means over (and hopefully never will be); the days of the incompetent amateur are numbered in today's funding climate.

Your reputation

Show how you have widespread support and goodwill throughout the community. Also, show how your users think really well of your work.

Your track record

Show how you have successfully done similar work in the past, or that you have set up other projects which have gone really well. In other words, what does the history of your organisation say about its likely future? Does it show that you have stumbled from crisis to crisis? If so, there is every reason to expect that this will continue. Or have you grown and developed or simply maintained a high quality of service? Then the funder will take great confidence from this.

Here are some things you can do:

1. Get comments and commendations from users and experts

- **Keep copies of any letters** you receive from grateful clients and users. Use selected parts to make up a 'quotes sheet' where a range of people say really positive things about you.
- **Evaluate your work**, either internally or through a formal external evaluation, and make a note of the key points from the evaluation which will enhance your credibility.
- **Ask experts** and others to visit you, and then ask them to write to you with their impressions of your work. Then ask them if you can use selected quotations in your fundraising proposals.

2. Get written about or reported in the local, specialist or national press or media

■ **Keep copies of any press coverage.** If you are a national organisation you may want to use a press cuttings agency to send you copies of any coverage you receive.

■ **Circulate copies** (or a collage of all the media coverage you have received) to supporters, potential supporters and key contacts where appropriate.

■ **Alert supporters** to forthcoming media coverage, especially phone-ins, and try to ensure that your voice is heard.

■ **Tape (or videotape) any radio or TV coverage** you get. It may prove useful as part of a presentation.

3. Keep in touch with existing funders

■ **Say 'thank you' promptly** for any support you have received. It is surprising how often recipients of grants fail to do this. And if you forget to, it can completely ruin your chances of getting further support.

■ **Send copies of your annual report**, and any other literature you produce which you feel may be of interest, even if you are not asking for money now. You want to try and show the funder that you are committed to building a long-standing relationship with them rather than simply asking for money when the last lot has run out.

■ **Send progress reports** and a **final report** on the project. Some of this you may be obliged to do under the terms of your grant. Try to show what you have been able to achieve with their money – outcomes as well as outputs.

■ **Suggest a visit** if they are in the area, or invite them to an 'open day' or other similar event. And make sure the organisation shows itself at its best.

■ **Build an informal working relationship.** If you are at the same conference, go up and introduce yourself. If there is anything you need to know or want to discuss, telephone them – but don't waste their time.

■ **Ensure that all queries and correspondence are answered promptly** and that telephone calls are received competently and cheerfully.

4. Get known to potential funders

Much of the above is also relevant to building relationships with potential funders, who you believe might be interested in your work and in supporting it now or in the future. Often it will be far better to develop your credibility with potential funders before approaching them for support. This means you need to get together a target list now. This will include all those you expect to apply to over the next five years or so. Put them on the list to receive your annual report, favourable press cuttings, invitations to your annual general meeting or evening receptions, or whatever seems appropriate.

When you first contact them on this basis, explain that you are not asking for money now, but that you hope they will be interested in your work and might want to support you at some point in the future. This does two things:

- **breaks the ice** when you actually get round to writing for money;
- **shows that you are committed to a partnership** with the funder. You are not one of those who simply asks for cash and is not heard from again until you want more.

You never know, you may even spark an idea in the funder which encourages them to approach you!

5. Know who your contacts are

You may well have contacts with trustees or administrators of grant sources, yet may not be aware of these. Draw up a list of potential funding sources and discuss them with your staff, trustees or management committee, your patrons and other prominent supporters. Find out who knows whom and how best such contacts might be mobilised in your support.

6. Bring people into your organisation

- as **patrons, vice-presidents**
- as **expert advisers**
- onto **specialist subcommittees** (events, fundraising etc.)
- as **trustees**.

You need such people as much for their contacts and fundraising credibility as for the practical help they can offer the organisation. In fact, someone with good contacts can save you hours and hours of painstaking reputation-building. So if you want to raise money from local business, try recruiting a prominent and popular local businessperson into your organisation and get them to do the fundraising on your behalf (as long as you make it clear to them from the start that this is what they are expected to do).

7. Build your credibility into your fundraising proposals

- **State on your letterhead who your patrons, trustees** and other prominent people associated with you are.
- **Mention the major support or sponsorship received** (particularly from government sources and other trusts and companies). If they have supported you, it shows that you are well-regarded.
- **Use impartial comments and commendations** from users and **mention any press or media coverage** in your proposal (or as an attachment to the written application). These show others endorsing what you are doing.
- **Mention your achievements** and your successes.

Credibility for new organisations

Credibility generally comes with your good track record, but if you are new – or relatively new – you don't really have one. So what can new organisations do to demonstrate their credibility?

- Talk about the expertise of all those involved in the work.

- Show the calibre of people you have as staff, management committee members, patron, vice presidents, project advisory group or whoever.

- Get letters of support and endorsement from a range of key people and agencies.

- Demonstrate by the quality of your business and project planning that you have seen a clear need, are capable of delivering an effective solution and have thought through a sensible and clear funding plan into the long term.

- Show that the project is based on a successful model developed elsewhere, although you have modified it slightly to adapt to the particular circumstances you face.

- Try and get some early press coverage about why the project is needed and what you hope to achieve.

All you are trying to do is give the funder the confidence that you know what you want to do and how you want to do it, that other people think it's worthwhile and that you are confident of succeeding. Some or all of the above should ensure you do achieve this.

---

8. Keep a credibility fact file

Buy a box file to keep all the press cuttings, commendation letters etc. that you may then want to use in your fundraising proposals.

See also Worksheets 2 and 3 – Credibility Fact File and Credibility Box File – in Chapter 10.

Financial credibility

You must show that your organisation is secure, solvent and makes good use of its funds. Your accounts, which many donors require a copy of, can give hidden messages, such as those listed below.

- That you are **flush with funds** or running a huge surplus, so you don't really need the money.
- That you are **out of financial control**, with expenditure consistently exceeding income, so you can't be trusted with money.
- That you are **spending too much on fundraising**, administration or travel, wasting the money you are given.

You may even have a qualified auditor's report, saying that the accounts do not present a true and fair view of your financial position (in the auditor's opinion). This can be a disaster.

On the other hand, your financial accounts may not fully reflect the extent of your work. This will particularly be the case if you receive a good deal of support in kind or through the efforts of volunteers. These inputs may not be included in the financial accounts, and yet this support is important.

If your accounts (as they are currently presented) will make the work of fundraising more difficult, you will need to address this before you start. It may often only be a matter of presentation, getting your accountant or auditor to agree to present the figures in a different way, to set aside provisions for future expenditure, or to add explanatory notes to the accounts. Or there may be a more fundamental problem which you will need to address before you can seriously begin the task of fundraising.

Remember, if there is a problem, explain what it is and how you are already moving towards a solution. Don't just pretend it doesn't exist.

Success and failure

Nothing succeeds like success! Funders like to back winners, not losers. If you can demonstrate a track record of success, this is likely to improve your fundraising chances.

What do you think are your real successes and achievements over the last two or three years which could usefully lend credibility to a fundraising application?

- **Successes relating to the organisation** as a whole?
- **Successful projects, events, work?**
- **Individual case study examples** of success (disguised if confidentiality is required)?
- **Success in attracting support** or sponsorship?
- **Objectives that have been achieved?**

Learn from failure

Although everyone wants to be successful, even the best-run organisations fail from time to time. Sometimes the project is experimental and simply does not work. Perhaps circumstances or needs will change. Occasionally a grant will be cut or further funding will fail to materialise. Sometimes it is due to circumstances beyond your control.

Whatever the reasons for failure, be honest about your achievements. Trumpet your successes by all means, but don't necessarily hide your failures. There may be lessons to be learned, experience to be disseminated, credibility to be won from explaining why the project didn't work out quite as planned.

List your successes

List six recent successes in your organisation. Get other people in the organisation (project workers, trustees, the accountant, a committed volunteer) to list six – do the lists match up?

1.
2.
3.
4.
5.
6.

■ **Exercise: Estimating the value of non-cash support**

For last year, estimate the following:

Value of items donated in kind

items   replacement cost

_____

_____

_____

_____

_____

Value of volunteer time

number of volunteers:

total hours of volunteer time valued on an hourly basis: £   per hour

total value of volunteer time: £

Remember to include *all* the volunteer inputs into your organisation. You can value volunteer time at the average wage, the minimum wage, the estimated cost of paying for the time or some notional – but reasonable – figure.

Value of secondments

valued on a similar basis to volunteers

NB: Were gifts in kind, volunteer time or secondments mentioned in your last year's annual accounts? Do they represent a significant proportion of your last year's total income? If the answer to the first question was *no* and the second question *yes*, what are you going to do about it?

These are the basic building ingredients of a good application. Having got this information together, you need to try and stand back a little and look at your application from a slightly different viewpoint to see if you make a good application into an even better one. The following chapter tries to shift the emphasis away from the information you need to assemble to the perspective you need to have.

■ Exercise: Judging your financial credibility

Get hold of a copy of your organisation's annual accounts for the last three years. Study carefully the *Income and Expenditure Account,* the *Balance Sheet* and the *Notes to the Accounts.* Jot down some of the positive and negative points that emerge from these figures.

On the plus side

On the minus side

Main problem areas to explain

3 Improving the Application

Having got together all the basic ingredients of a good application, you now need to stand back a little and bring some new thinking to bear on the applications process. This should enable you to present your work in a way that grabs the donor's attention and helps your application stand out from the crowd.

Think in project terms

The whole purpose of fundraising is getting hold of enough money to meet the day-to-day and capital expenditure that your organisation is incurring, plus the resources required for its future development.

But it is far easier to raise money for something specific than for the organisation as a whole. This is because donors can then match the support they give to some specific piece of work or expenditure, to a particular activity or outcome. They will feel that their money is actually doing something.

So, rather than just asking supporters to make a generous contribution to your organisation or its overall financial needs, it is best to ask them to support a particular aspect of your work or to pay for a specific item of expenditure.

Thinking of your work in project terms and designing projects which will attract support is the basis of successful fundraising and proposal writing.

There's no such thing as core funding!

Charities often say they can get funding for projects or for capital spending but not for their administrative or core costs.

To tackle this, the first step is to eliminate these core costs as a separate item from your thinking. You do not have any costs other than those which are necessary for carrying out your work or projects. If you do you are breaking the law, because a charity can only spend money wholly and exclusively on its charitable purposes.

So, you need to:

- think of your work as a series of projects
- build your full overhead costs into each of these activities
- recognise that if the overhead costs have not been paid for, the project is not fully funded.

For more information on how to do this, see Chapter 4 on Costing a Project.

This immediately raises the question of how you get support for those parts of your work which are unlikely to be attractive to donors. There are a number of possible ways of overcoming this problem.

- **Use your core grants and general fundraising income** to pay for the administration costs or the parts of your work it is especially difficult to raise money for.
- **Cost all your projects realistically.** Include all the expenditure you are likely to incur. This is dealt with further in Chapter 4 on Costing a Project.
- **Include an allocation of overhead costs** in your project budget. It is reasonable that every project should make an appropriate contribution to the general costs of running the organisation. This allocation should be made on some suitable basis which you are prepared to justify, rather than a figure plucked out of the air (see also Chapter 4).
- **Be creative** in how you match your income to your expenditure. Be realistic in how you cost your projects. Be imaginative in designing attractive projects to raise money for.

The problem can arise that your fundraising for one particular project is so successful that you have raised more than you need or can reasonably spend on the work. What do you then do?

You must do something. If you have asked for money for a particular purpose, then you are obliged to spend it on that purpose. You will have to go back to at least some of your supporters and ask if you can spend their grant on another project or for another purpose. They will almost certainly agree to this. Or you might decide to expand the project or allocate the surplus to next year's expenditure; again, you should keep your supporters informed.

Difficulties arise when fundraising threatens to determine the work of the organisation. Many organisations find that it is easy to raise money for a particular purpose, and then re-organise themselves to fit in with this. Ideally, you should first decide what you want the organisation to do and then raise money for that. There will inevitably be some trade-off between what you can easily raise money for and what you want to be doing, but you should try to keep the two in a reasonable balance. Otherwise the organisation will lose purpose and direction.

Where you judge the project to be unattractive for fundraising, you will need to think carefully. It will be a waste of your time to seek funds for something that is unlikely to appeal to donors. In such circumstances, you might:

- find a way of restructuring, refocusing, or representing the project so that it appears more attractive to donors;

- think of something else to raise money for, which will be more attractive. Most organisations can juggle their budgets so that the more attractive projects are put forward for fundraising and the remainder of the money comes through the general fundraising income it is receiving;
- discuss whether there are alternative ways of financing the project (e.g. through charging fees for services or developing a new income stream). Many people tend to be rather grants obsessed. Always ask yourself whether short-term grants are the only or the best way.

Making a project more fundable

Once you have decided on a project which you are going to raise money for, the next step is to see whether and how you can make it more attractive to donors. Donors will certainly want to see value for their money, and possibly some long-term impact on the organisation they are investing in. This improvement process will also allow you to think through what you are doing, and even help you create a better project – which is an added benefit.

> **A fundable project should be:**
>
> - specific – an identifiable item of expenditure or aspect of the organisation's work
> - important – both to the organisation and to the cause or need it is meeting. If there is some long-term impact, that will be an added bonus
> - effective – there should be a clear and positive outcome
> - realistic – the work proposed should be achievable
> - good value – the work should be a good use of the donor's money
> - topical – it should be looking at current issues and concerns
> - relevant – it should be relevant to the donor and the donor's particular funding concerns
> - bite-sized – it should not be too large or too small for a donor to support, although the cost might be shared through several smaller grants. If it is too large, it might be broken down further into sub-projects.

Grant-winning ideas and fundable projects

What is a good idea? A good idea is something that will have immediate appeal with donors as being different, lively, worthwhile and worth funding. The donor's first response is more likely to be 'Gosh, that sounds good; we ought to be backing that', rather than, 'I've had ten applications like that in the last month, and none of them are likely to achieve very much'.

Good ideas are central to good fundraising. Even the very best application may not make up for a poorly thought-out project or for something that simply is not very interesting. However, it is difficult to define what constitutes a good idea. Usually it is something that leaps out at you from the page, and seems obvious once someone has thought of it. The following are some ingredients of a good idea.

- It meets a **really important and urgent need.**
- It is **fresh or interesting** (or at least sounds it) and captures the imagination.
- It is – or sounds – **startlingly obvious**, even though nobody has thought of it before.

Assessing the fundability of a project

A Case Study: The Big Step

The Big Step, established in July 1996, is the charitable arm of *The Big Issue in the North*. *The Big Issue* is the magazine sold by homeless vendors which enables them to earn a legitimate income and so begin the difficult journey into employment.

The Big Step's aim is to enable the vendors to achieve their ambitions and escape the trap of homelessness. This is done by creating for each vendor on The Big Step Programme an individualised plan which addresses all the obstacles in the way of a new life: accommodation, health care, drug/alcohol abuse, training and employment. Some services are bought in but others, particularly employment training, will be done in-house.

For the financial year, The Big Step will need funding for the following projects/posts:
1. A new headquarters for the magazine business and the charity.
2. An Employment Unit for vendors on The Big Step Programme.
3. A computer database to manage donor information and mailings.
4. An annual report.
5. Publicity brochures for The Big Step for vendors and the general public.
6. A quarterly newsletter for the Friends of The Big Issue.
7. Big Step caseworker posts (x 6).
8. Service Development Managers (x 4).
9. Researcher.

- Which do you think are the easiest to raise money for?
- Where would you go for money for each of these projects?
- What would each funder be looking to achieve through their support?

A fundable project: The Employment Unit

The Big Step wants to set up a unit which will assist vendors and drug users to achieve their potential and to gain employment or set up their own small business.

Why? Homeless people and drug users need intensive support and training if they are to compete for jobs. *The Big Issue in the North*'s experience is that existing agencies are unable or unwilling to cater for long-term homeless people or those using street drugs. Hence the need for the Employment Unit.

Such a unit is potentially very attractive to a range of funders in both the public and private sectors for the following reasons:

- Costs and outcomes are clear.
- Costs can be broken down into distinct elements (a computer plus software package, for example) or the project can be taken as a whole.
- The end is highly socially desirable – alienation among young people is fast rising up the political and social agenda.
- There is a clear economic case for the project as it attempts to tackle the very difficult area of long-term unemployment.
- It is sustainable. Once the project has demonstrated its effectiveness it will be able to generate training contracts from TECs and obtain on-going European funding.
- Given that it costs the taxpayer over £9,000 a year per unemployed person, a successful project will represent real value for money.
- The range of funders it was able to approach (the project became part of a successful

continued ...

joint SRB bid as well as the recipient of considerable trust funding) meant that each funder saw a good return on its own investment.

- The organisation was able to contribute some funding itself through its *Friends* organisation.
- The project was able to raise the money in stages. For example, a single trust was successfully sounded out privately to fund the entire capital costs. This meant that by the time it wanted to approach other funders with whom it had a less established relationship, it was well on the way to meeting its target. This would be a great encouragement to these funders.

The cost of the unit in Year One were as follows:

Capital

Computers and software	£35,000
Furniture	£10,000

Revenue

Recruitment costs	£5,000
Unit Manager	£20,976
Trainers	£19,706
Training	£12,000
College/TEC fees	£8,000
Travel	£1,250
Telephone	£2,000
Publications	£500
Misc	£1,000
Total costs	*£115,432*

Finally, all 'core' or central costs were donated by *The Big Issue*. Again, this is another major plus point which adds to the level of return on each donor's contribution.

- It has a **catchy title**.
- It is or appears **innovative**.
- It is **topical** – it fits within current fashions, thinking, concerns.
- It is **different** – it stands out in the crowd of more ordinary applications.
- It has **different aspects** which appeal to different funding constituencies (wide appeal).
- It shows **value for money** or **leverage** (a small input with lots and lots of output).
- It **complements and supplements existing provision** or involves collaboration with other agencies.
- It has **measurable objectives** and specific outcomes which are clearly of benefit.
- It is **realistic** and **achievable**.
- It is **fundable**, and may even **develop its own income** in the long term.

Examples of good ideas

1. The National Pyramid Trust

This trust's method of work was developed in Hounslow schools with initial funding from the Economic and Social Research Council. It is a preventative system for helping 7-8 year old schoolchildren at risk of later educational and social failure. Using a previously proven 'therapeutic group' model, the principal innovation is to train volunteers – mostly students – to run the groups, thereby making them affordable within existing budgets for all children that can benefit.

The National Pyramid Trust was founded to spread its system of prevention on a national basis. Start-up funding came from a small family trust interested in innovative work with vulnerable children. Early support from the Gulbenkian Foundation took the form of a small lunch-time meeting for the most likely potential funders, both from government and from trusts, at which the scheme was presented and discussed in detail. Almost all those invited subsequently became substantial funders.

Two pilot projects in new areas were supported and, following their successful transfer to on-going local funding, the trust has now moved to a full three-year development programme with trust, government and lottery support.

2. The Youth Charter for Sport

This project works particularly with young people in Moss Side in Manchester. Run by a former world karate champion, the project has used sports celebrities to get the interest and attention of highly disaffected young people. This has given the project credibility among a much greater range of funders. For example, many companies like to be associated with sporting celebrities and the project has capitalised on this. The project calculates that it has brought in over £1 million of resources into Moss Side in its first three years. It continues to build on its sporting links to encourage young people to find a new way in life. Indeed, the 1997 South African Football team visited the Proctor Youth Centre (a YCS flagship project) before an international match. There is nothing new about wishing to work with disaffected young people; however, YCS's use of sport, and the intense personal charisma of the chairman, gives it a freshness and radicalism that compels both the young people and the funders.

How to develop good ideas

Respond to need as it emerges. You are at the front line of social provision. The needs you identify will be met by the established services of tomorrow.

Two heads are better than one. Get together with colleagues to 'brainstorm' ideas. Or just wallow in a warm bath!

Keep an eye on the 'marketplace' – see what others are doing. Keep in touch with social trends, fashions and fads.

Write down ideas as soon as you have thought of them, however half-baked or ill thought-out they appear. If you don't, you'll forget them. If you do, you can develop and refine them over time.

Bring in outsiders who have no preconceptions. This can provide a degree of 'lateral thinking' which will be useful. You know how the buses or the health service should be run, so it is a good bet that outsiders can teach you a thing or two. Stop thinking about what you can't do and about 'all the problems and difficulties'. Develop a positive can-do attitude to your work and your organisation.

Go back to basics. Forget what you do now. What should you be doing in the ideal world? Look at your organisation's objects or purposes as enshrined in the founding documents and think about the problems/ needs and what you would do if starting from scratch.

Somewhere, there is an idea which is just right for your organisation, which will be easy to raise money for, which will enhance your credibility and public image, and which (hopefully) will solve all your financial problems… for ever.

> ■ **Exercise**
>
> Go round the organisation and get a list of 20 things that colleagues want funded. Rank them in terms of fundability. Do they form the basis of a good fundraising programme?

Adding value

Wherever possible, try to show the funder that you are giving and getting maximum value from their support. Investment, leverage, dissemination and evaluation are all useful concepts in this process

1. Investment

An investment is an expenditure which builds the potential of the organisation and helps it move towards a more successful future. It aims to build a more secure and successful organisation later on rather than simply provide a service now. It can be an extremely important and cost-effective way of providing support. Some possibilities are listed below.

- **Investing in capacity:** to enable you to undertake more work more effectively or to earn more money from the services you provide.
- **Investing in efficiency:** to streamline the organisation and cut waste.
- **Investing in training and skills:** to improve the quality and effectiveness of your work.
- **Investing in plant or equipment:** for example, buying a piece of equipment to improve your efficiency or effectiveness.
- **Investing in fundraising:** for example, developing a supporter group which over time will generate increased income.
- **Investing in long-term stability:** for example, generating the resources or information which will enable you to negotiate contracts and service agreements which will underpin your future financial security.

All these can be the subject of a fundraising application. Indeed, you can often put a gloss on events which make them appear to be more planned and thought out than they in fact were. If you realise that you are currently short of money and have ideas for future income generation, you could dress this up as a stage one/stage two proposal. This is where you show how you have reached the end of one phase of your development and you need to get to the next stage; you ask for funding to help you get from where you are to where you need to be.

2. Leverage

Leverage is the process whereby a small amount of support helps create a large amount of impact. This is the ideal position for a donor, so showing leverage can improve your chances of success. There are many ways in which this can be done.

- **Matching grants:** where one donor has promised to pay half the costs if you can raise the rest. Every pound you now raise will release an additional pound of the donor's money. This is often used by companies when they match their employees' fundraising activities pound for pound.

- **Challenge grants:** where you ask a donor to promise a certain sum of money on the condition that you raise the rest by a certain date. This gives the donor the assurance that their promise of money is being used to lever other sums, and the confidence that if you fail to raise the outstanding amounts the original donor owes nothing.

- **Fundraising leverage:** where the support given will enable you to raise a much larger sum. A prize offered for a raffle, for example, may enable you to raise a considerable sum through selling raffle tickets. Or integrated software would allow you to develop a membership and alumni programme worth £X hundred thousand pounds a year.

- **Use of volunteers:** the value of the work done can be very much larger if volunteers rather than paid staff are used.

- **Discounts:** obtaining discounts on purchases or even getting items on your budget donated free shows an effective organisation and allows the donor's contribution to go that much further.

- **Problem solving:** by meeting the need now you then save money which would otherwise have to be spent dealing with the consequences (e.g. by stopping young people turning to crime).

3. Dissemination

People will be interested in the impact of your work, and its effect in alleviating the problem. If the money is to undertake research or produce a publication, they will want to be told how the research findings will be disseminated or how the publication will be distributed. If the money is for some form of innovation or a pilot project, they will want to be shown how the success of the project will be measured and what will be done subsequently to promote the lessons learned and encourage others to replicate the ideas.

Dissemination can be linked to the concept of leverage. For example, a locally run project can be copied throughout the country if it can be shown to be effective, so £X thousand pounds given to you means that ultimately the whole country can benefit.

The application for funds is just the first part of the process. Obtaining the money and undertaking the work outlined in the proposal is the second stage. The third stage is to make use of the outcome in some way, and where this is an important ingredient of the proposal it should be fully discussed in the application.

4. Evaluation

Increasingly funders require the organisations they support to produce some sort of evaluation of the outcome of their work. This means setting measurable objectives for your project and then measuring the results you achieve, whether this is the number of people attending your activities or changes in attitude or behaviour towards the problem. Evaluation is particularly important for the National Lottery Charities Board.

Many applications are disappointingly vague about what they will actually do and how they will measure progress. The key thing is firstly to set some measurable targets, and secondly to show how discussions about progress will be fed into the management of the project (and, indeed, the management of the organisation). There is little point saying: 'We are behind (or ahead) of our targets' and then proceed to do nothing about it. Monitoring and evaluation is about action and decision-making. You need to show who will take action and when.

This will not only demonstrate how effective you are – and if you can do this you will find it that much easier to obtain funding in the future – but it will also provide you with a tool to manage your project, to make the appropriate changes and adjustments as the work proceeds.

Some evaluation can cost a good deal of money (e.g. for professional consultancy, surveys and other market research, or the work involved in the measurement of outcomes). From time to time, it may be appropriate for an organisation to undertake a serious evaluation with the aim of setting the stage for its future development. Indeed the costs of this can be packaged up into a 'project' and be the subject of a fundraising application. But evaluation need not cost money if it is thought through and built into the way the project is run right from the start. Evaluation of what you do shows a professional approach, and in a competitive world, this can only be an advantage.

Chapters 2 and 3 have looked at what you need to put into an application and how you can give it the fundraising edge. Having decided on what you want to apply for, the next thing to look at is how to make sure you are asking for the right amount of money.

4 Costing a Project

The budget

The budget is a central element of your application. It sets out your financial need and provides the base around which your argument for support is developed.

People are often frightened by the budgeting process. They give it an aura and mystique that it simply does not have, and wrongly assume that it is a skill possessed only by the privileged few. Budgeting is no more than a careful costing of all the items of expenditure involved in the work you are proposing. But since many of the items cannot be precisely determined or allocated, there is plenty of scope for creativity in coming to a final figure for your fundraising.

A common mistake is for people to under-cost their budgets. Perhaps they feel that if they apply for less, they stand a better chance of getting the money. But if you always apply for too little, you will end up in a financial mess.

It is better to go for a larger sum when raising money, particularly where the project is well thought through and likely to be attractive to donors. You will then be concentrating your effort on the fundraising which is most likely to succeed. By including overhead costs and allowing for other costs which you might have otherwise omitted, you will be bringing money into your organisation which you would otherwise have to raise in other ways. The trick is to demonstrate the benefits of the project and how much will be achieved by the work – rather than showing how little it will cost to do it.

> **Stages in the budget process**
>
> 1. Describe the project
> 2. Write down the expenditure needs
> 3. Cost each item as carefully as you can
> 4. Total the costs
> 5. Examine the total and amend the budget if necessary
> 6. Agree the budget.

The budgeting process

There are basically six elements in the budgeting process. Here are two examples of different kinds of projects, one mainly capital, the second mainly revenue. They follow through the same six stages.

Example 1 – Buying a computer

Stage 1

Describe in detail the scope of the project and what you intend to do with the money. Compare the following statements:

- we plan to buy a computer;
- we plan to computerise our membership and mailing lists through the purchase of a computer.

These are two very different fundraising propositions. The first simply involves the purchase of equipment. The second is about using the equipment to advance the organisation and its work. It involves additional costs and will be more expensive, but it is also likely to be more attractive to donors.

This applies to any kind of capital or equipment purchase. "We want to buy a building" or "We need a minibus" are pretty dull statements. "We want to release the creative talents of our young people by setting up a community arts centre", or "We want to overcome the problems of rural isolation by bringing older people together twice a week" are much more engaging. It's not about your needs, it's about your users' needs. Talk about them, not you.

Stage 2

Write down a list of all the budget heads of expenditure. Then think if you have left anything out. Here is a possible list for a computerisation project.

- Computer hardware
- Peripheral equipment
- Installation costs
- Furniture
- Software
- Software development and consultancy
- Staff training and induction
- Transfer of existing records
- Stationery (first year's supply)
- Maintenance contract
- Sundry and contingency costs (e.g. cost of attending courses and conferences, purchase of publications, registration under Data Protection Act).

Stage 3

Cost each item using the best estimates you can.

- **Computer hardware:** quote prices before discount. Any discount you get can be treated as fundraising.

- **Transfer of records:** you will need to transfer your existing 5,000 records onto the new machine at (say) 50p per record.
- **Staff training and induction:** you will need to ensure your staff can operate the new system confidently and efficiently. This will include not just the cost of sending staff on training courses, but any time spent or wasted in staff getting to know the system and learning to use it effectively.
- **Stationery:** although this is an application for a one-off project, and stationery is more of a running cost, it would be perfectly reasonable to include the purchase of one year's supply of stationery (and maybe even the design costs of having stationery produced with your organisation's name and details) in this application.

Stage 4

Add up the estimated costs to create a total budget for the project

Item	£
Hardware	1,900
Peripherals	500
Installation	100
Furniture	500
Software	500
Consultancy (provisional)	1,500
Staff training & induction	3,000
Transfer of records	2,500
Stationery	850
Maintenance contract	300
Sundry	350
Total	**12,000**

Stage 5

Examine the total to decide whether it provides a reasonable basis for your fundraising. Is the end figure you have arrived at too high, too low or about right? It is perfectly possible to re-cost the project so that the total comes out substantially higher or substantially lower. Many of the items are simply best guesses at this stage, and only time will tell; some you will never be able to put an exact figure on, even when you have finished the work. For example, how much unproductive time will your staff be spending before the system is running smoothly? You would never find that out, but have included this in your £3,000 for staff training – it could be costed at more or less.

Changing the way in which the figures are calculated can have a very real effect on the end result. For example, rather than charging 50p per record transfer, charge 40p or 60p or whatever. You can also take out part of the project, or add on another item of expenditure (for example paying for some market research on your membership) in order to arrive at a different figure.

Do you think that the project represents value for money? Concentrate your thinking on the benefits rather than the costs of the project. In the example given, you could show that by introducing the system, you will develop your fundraising, expand your membership, and improve your overall efficiency. You can even set targets for this to show that the £12,000 you are seeking is not only value for money, but also an essential building block in your organisation's future. Attach a basic three-year plan which shows how this computer system will save £20,000 a year in administrative costs and will, by year 3, be helping generate an additional £30,000 a year in new members (because of the recruitment drive it will enable you to embark upon).

Is the total required too much for one particular donor to support? If so, approach several donors. You can even break down the project into bite-sized chunks, asking one donor to contribute the computer, another the installation etc.

Stage 6

You now have a final, agreed budget for the project. This is the target for your fundraising, and the basis on which you can create a fundraising plan.

Example 2 - An outreach project

Often it is not simply a question of calculating the direct costs of a project. Sometimes you will want to include an allocation of overheads or a contribution to your organisation's central administration costs, especially when applying for salaries and other revenue funding. This is a perfectly reasonable thing to do. The basis on which these costs are apportioned will vary from project to project, but it should be based on a sensible apportionment of the costs. It is the same six-stage process. (To avoid repetition, we are only expanding on points which are particularly relevant to revenue applications – otherwise the points made in the computer example above are all valid.)

Stage 1 – Describe the project

We wish to help people out of poverty and to take more control over their lives by helping them achieve greater financial independence. We will do this by establishing a new money advice project.

Stage 2 – Write down the expenditure

- Salary/National Insurance of money advice worker
- Basic equipment needs (new desk, computer etc.)

- Premises costs (rent, rates, heat, light, cleaning etc.)
- Post, telephone, stationery etc.
- Central costs (insurance, bank charges, accountancy, audit etc.)
- Management/supervision
- Volunteer expenses
- Clerical support
- Travel

Charities often say that they can get funding for project or for capital spending, but not for their administrative or core costs. The key to overcoming this is to eliminate these core costs as a separate item in your thinking. You do not have any core costs. The only costs you carry are those which are necessary for undertaking your work, unless you have people who do absolutely nothing. Therefore, you need to build these full overhead costs into all your activities and recognise that unless they have been funded the project has not been funded.

Putting down all the direct costs is usually a fairly straightforward process. The difficult part can be remembering all those hidden costs which are vital to the project's success but which are far less obvious (e.g. occupying the building, management and central costs). However, make sure you get them all down.

> *There's no such thing as "core costs"! All your costs are spent on the work you do. Therefore, make sure you build all relevant overhead costs into each "project" application you make.*

Stage 3 – Cost each item

Again, the direct costs are fairly easy to put a figure on. You know the expected salary of the worker. You know what kind of basic equipment he or she will need. However, how do you calculate the central costs?

The most common way of calculating central costs is to look at the percentage of space the person will take up and the office facilities he or she will share. For example, if the outreach worker will use one fifth of the office building, allocate one fifth of the premises costs (rent, rates, heat, light etc.) to the project. If the outreach worker shares office facilities equally with eight other full-time workers, allocate one eighth of the post, telephone, stationery and other such bills. If the outreach project occupies a quarter of the manager's time in terms of development, support and supervision, allocate a quarter of the manager's salary and national insurance to the project.

In the end, all you are trying to achieve is a realistic figure for the cost to the organisation as a whole of running this new project. It is not a fiddle. You are not trying quietly to bump up the figures and apply for more

---

Thinking things through

A director of a major grant-making trust was recently asked whether she had noticed any major changes in the applications she had been receiving since the introduction of the National Lottery Charities Board. "Not really", she replied. She went on to say that she thought things would change from the summer of 1998 when the first grants cycle started coming to an end. However, she said that she had received an interesting application recently, which ran along the following lines: "We have been awarded a National Lottery Charities Board grant to run XXX project. This involves taking on three new workers, all of whom are funded by the Charities Board. However, we now need someone to manage these workers. Will you (the grant-making trust) pay for the salary costs of this manager?" A classic case of an under-funded project!

than you should. Rather, you are simply aiming to avoid the position whereby you suddenly find the telephone bill has risen substantially on account of this new project and you cannot meet the extra cost.

Stage 4 – Total the costs

Total the costs up on the above basis. Make sure that you explain how you have arrived at the costs in notes to your budget, as follows:

Salary & National Insurance	£16,500
Premises costs *	£8,200
Supervision and support +	£7,500
Volunteer expenses #	£6,000
Other	£6,800
TOTAL	£45,000

Notes

* = 20% of occupancy costs

\+ = 25% of management and 12.5% of admin salaries

\# = X volunteers per week at Y travel/expenses and Z training costs

Stage 5

When looking at the overall costs, again you can change them if you are not happy with them. Re-assess the resources required by the project and adjust the percentages you have used accordingly. Remember you may be asked to justify the basis of your calculations, so they have got to appear reasonable.

Also, if you already have a grant which covers some or all of your central costs (say from your local authority), you can use this to show that you have already covered some of the costs of the project. Therefore, ifthe above budget comes to £45,000 a year; you can show that you have already raised £15,000 of this from existing resources. It is important that you do this for three reasons:

(i) It demonstrates to the funder that you have not forgotten anything. If you simply leave these costs out because they have already been paid for, then the funder may get the impression that you haven't thought the project through properly.

(ii) The hardest part of your fundraising is getting the fundraising ball rolling. Once you have started getting money in, other funders take confidence from this and pledge their support accordingly. So if you can show that some of the required money is already there, this gives the whole thing an impetus that it otherwise would not have.

(iii) Some funders, notably the National Lottery Charities Board, are saying explicitly that they will not pay for costs which are already covered by another grant. So you need to show clearly which part of the project falls into which category. But again, having some of the project paid for already gives a bit of leverage to your application because the new funder only has to give £XXX to make this wonderful work happen.

Stage 6 – Agree the budget

As with the example of the computer above, you should now be clear where the money for the different parts of the organisation's costs are coming from, as well as having an agreed fundraising plan. This kind of project fundraising can feel a bit like being a juggler and keeping lots of different fundraising balls in the air at the same time. The advantage is that if you can do it, you broaden your fundraising scope and become less dependent on a single funder.

Common mistakes in budgeting

Forgotten costs

Have you included **all** the items you will be spending money on? What about training and attending courses? Buying necessary publications? Travel and subsistence? Who is going to pay for these if you don't raise the money? Or will this extra expenditure just increase your deficit?

Hidden costs

Every project consumes office space, heating, lighting, telephone, postage, the cost of supervision by the director and the committee of management. You need to include a reasonable element of them in your budget for the project. Since it is far easier to raise money for projects than it is for administration or running the office, by allocating your overhead costs onto your projects, you will use the glamour of the project to get the unattractive administrative costs paid for.

Understated costs

It is easy to put too low a cost in your budget. There are several reasons for this. There is a tendency to underestimate the costs of the project because you think that the fundraising will be difficult. Or you may be basing your estimate on this year's costs, or worse, on last year's, but your budget is for next year when inflation will have increased the cost of everything. Get as good an estimate as possible for the cost of each item and allow something for inflation.

When you are applying for a grant over several years, you can either allow for inflation on an estimated basis for the second and subsequent years (you would normally state the assumptions you have made in a footnote to the budget). Or you can calculate your budget on the first year's costs, and ask that an inflation adjustment be made as each year's instalment falls due.

If you leave out any item of expenditure from your budget or put in a cost which is less than what will actually be incurred, then you will be out of pocket. If you consistently do this, then you will have a financial problem. It also looks extremely bad from a fundraising point of view if you have to go back to a funder asking for more money simply because you under-estimated the costs.

Doing what you say you will do

If you say that you **will** do something, and you take money on that basis, then you **must** spend the money in the way you have proposed. If you can't, then you will have to discuss the situation with the donor, or return the money. Therefore, don't promise what you cannot deliver simply because it would make the proposal more attractive to the funder.

However, note the difference between actually stating that you will do something and indicating in a more general way how you plan to spend the money. For example, there is a clear difference between asking for and getting £200 to buy a specific piece of furniture (for your new building) and saying that £200 would purchase the piece of furniture. In the first case, if you get the money you have to buy the furniture; in the second case, unless the donor expressly states that the money is for the furniture, you can spend it for the more general purposes of your application. You have used the furniture to paint a picture of what the donation will achieve so as to make the fundraising that much easier.

Some donors may require you to spend the grant precisely as you have indicated in your budget, and require audited accounts demonstrating that you have done just this. Other donors are happy so long as you have spent the money roughly as detailed in the budget for the purposes set out in the application (they do not care if you have spent more on some items, less on others; they are more interested in the fact that the work you have proposed has actually been done). In any case your auditor will want to examine the basis on which the grants were received, and how the money was spent. You may want to check with the donor at the time you accept the grant what reporting arrangements (if any) will be required.

5 Improving Your Communication Skills

Writing in plain English

Faced with the task of writing an application, some people find it hard to put their thoughts together in a clear, logical way. Others develop a writer's block, so that although they have thought through what they want to say, they don't actually get round to putting anything in writing.

An application is no more than an answer to simple questions such as:

- Who you are
- What you currently do
- What you want to do
- Why this work is important
- What you need to enable you to do it
- How the donor can help you.

If you were answering these questions in conversation, you would become really enthusiastic. And in doing so, you would enthuse the person you were asking for money.

In your written application, you have to try to create this same sense of up-beat enthusiasm about your proposals as you would in conversation. Picture yourself chatting at a bar or over coffee, trying

---

A well-written application can make the difference

A well-written application will certainly improve your chances. You will not only have marshalled your ideas and the argument for supporting you in a more persuasive and readable way, but you will also have given the reader the impression that you are well-organised and capable; sufficiently so to be entrusted with their money as the following (true) story shows.

A friend (whom we shall call Paul) was raising money for a conference in Manchester in which homeless people would speak out about homelessness issues. He was jointly organising this with someone (Peter) who worked for a homelessness charity. They agreed that they would approach a major company based in the area and ask for support for the conference.

Peter organised a meeting with the company without telling Paul, who was putting together a written application. Peter rang Paul after the meeting to say not to bother putting an application in as the company wasn't interested. Paul said it was too late as he had already posted it. Paul got a phone call the next day to say that the company was putting in £1,500 to the conference. This was based purely on the fact that the application accurately reflected both a really exciting project and an understanding of the company's desire to be seen as a good corporate citizen.

---

to persuade someone of the importance of what you are doing and why they should give their support. That is what your written application is all about.

Other points to bear in mind.
1. You have to put down your thoughts in an ordered way, and be as clear and succinct as you can.
2. You have to make every word work for you as you have limited space and the attention span of the reader will be short.
3. Your application is being read along with hundreds of others each month. It has to be clearly set out and easy to read.

Some common writer's diseases

Verbicide

Using words whose meaning has been killed. Avoid using jargon, the words that only you and the professionals in your field know the meaning of. In an application you are usually talking to people who know little of the detail of what you are doing, and are unlikely to understand the specialist words which you take for granted.

'We believe that children, given the right environment, have an enormous, but often untapped, potential to learn. The concept of the learning organisation/company, in many ways, has now become commonplace. We believe that this concept, replicated in communities, could have significant benefits.'

What is a 'learning organisation' or 'learning company'? Although this is central to the application it is never explained. Therefore, unless the funder is an authority on educational issues they will not understand what the project is really about.

'Short-term respite care and flexible day care are the two most valuable forms of support for sufferers of Alzheimer's disease which allows the carer to cope longer in the community.'

What on earth does this mean? What is flexible day care and short term respite care? And why are they valuable? You may know the answers. Your readers (unless they are specialists in the caring business) are unlikely to.

Verbitis

Using inflamed words, such as unsubstantiated superlatives. Words and phrases such as 'desperate', 'unique', 'a major new initiative' have lost their meaning through over-use and should be avoided if possible. The reader will also be reading dozens of other applications all of which show desperate needs and unique solutions to the urgent problem. They want to know the facts and the figures, not the generalities expressed in the same meaningless superlatives.

Also, avoid the 'everybody knows' syndrome, where you make a bland statement on the assumption that the reader will understand its full significance. 'We all know that crime in general and youth crime in particular is on the increase. We also know that government initiatives to tackle these problems have failed.' Do we? In any case this doesn't convince the reader that you are particularly on top of your subject. If you can't show a deep understanding of the issues, how can you persuade the reader that you have a clearly workable solution.

'Our college is a unique institution in British higher education... Our facilities are woefully inadequate... We operate in a very desolate and most deprived area.'

This comes from a major university appeal in London. It raises more questions than answers. Be specific. Explain exactly what you mean. Why is the institution unique? Why are the facilities inadequate? Why is the area desolate? How deprived is it?

Verbosity

Just waffling on and on and on. You drown the meaning in a sea of useless words. Make every word work for you. Use a red pen to strike out what is meaningless, what adds nothing to your case. If there is very little left after doing this, then this gives you the opportunity to make a better case.

'Within our play centre, staff are required to enable us to register with Social Services and therefore operate within the law. A particularly high level of skill and understanding are needed in this sensitive area and therefore we feel it particularly useful to have the continuity of qualified staff to maintain the high level of confidence needed in the provision of this service, that is so vital to maintain free access to the centre.'

This paragraph is elaborating on the need for paid staff to run a play centre within a community education facility. Apart from the points that paid staff for the play centre are a requirement and that operating a play centre is essential to provide access to the facilities of the centre, how much of the rest of this paragraph is necessary?

■ Exercise

Rewrite the following sentences:

■ It would be our hope that you might fund this project.

■ A demonstrated commitment to co-operation and collaboration forms the cornerstone of this partnership.

■ This book was written on the understanding that it would provide...

■ We can assure you that any contribution you would be able to make would be used to...

■ Your grant has proved to be of great significance to this organisation, and we would like to express our gratitude.

Or look at the following supplied by the Plain English Campaign:

What on earth do these sentences mean?

1. 'Making a skill adjustment.'

2. 'Achieving a positive budget variance.'

3. 'Meaningful down turn in aggregate output.'

4. 'Grain-consuming animal units.'

5. 'An unselected roll-back to idle.'

6. 'Localised capacity deficiencies.'

7. 'High-quality learning environments are a necessary pre-condition for facilitation and enhancement of the on-going learning process.'

8. 'If there are any points on which you require explanation or further particulars we shall be glad to furnish such additional details as may be required by telephone.'

9. 'A device or arrangement that may be used to permit a patient to lie down when the need to do so is a consequence of the patient's condition rather than a need for active examination, diagnostic investigation, manipulative treatment, obstetric delivery or transport.'

10. 'Any resolution which, if carried, would, in the opinion of the chairman, substantially increase the expenditure upon any service which is under the management of or reduce the revenue at the disposal of any committee, or which would involve capital expenditure, shall, when proposed and seconded, stand adjourned without discussion to the next ordinary meeting of the council, and any committee affected by it shall consider whether it desires to report thereon.'

Answers

1.	Making a lot of staff redundant.	6.	Traffic bottlenecks.
2.	Making a lot of staff redundant.	7.	Children need good schools.
3.	A recession.	8.	Please ring if you have any questions.
4.	Farm animals such as cows, pigs or sheep.	9.	A bed.
5.	The plane's engine failed in mid-flight.	10.	The council's committees have no power over financial matters.

There are two further and extremely common means of padding out applications.

- Many organisations describe their structure along these lines: 'XXX is a registered charity and a voluntary organisation'. This is normally redundant information. It will be obvious from the nature of your work and your letterhead what your legal status is. A donor will only want to know if you are not a charity, as this can affect how the grant is paid over.
- Towards the end of the application, many people sign off with long-winded pleasantries, such as: 'I hope you will be able to give favourable consideration to our request for support and if you would like to discuss this initiative further or require more information, please do not hesitate to contact me at the above address.'

■ **Exercise**

Take a fundraising application you or a colleague have previously written, and rewrite it avoiding the four Vs – *verbicide, verbitis, verbosity* and *verbification*. Aim to cut its length by at least 25%.

Verbification

Producing a continuous stream of syllables where it could expressed more succinctly simply by tightening up your language.

- Avoid **longer words**, where shorter words will do:
  Not personal **motorised transportation**, but **private car**
  Not the **anticipated cost of the project**, but the **budget** for the project
- Avoid **long sentences**. Use punctuation to make the meaning clearer
- Avoid **long paragraphs**, which can become unreadable
- Aim for a **tabloid** rather than broadsheet style.

Some practical next steps

- **Buy yourself a red pen**. Use it to shorten and tighten up the next application you write, a **highlighter** to note the points that are unclear, badly explained or where more information is needed, and a pencil to make marginal notes.
- **Find yourself a journalist** – possibly on your local newspaper. They are used to writing for popular consumption and fitting what they want to say into a limited space. Perhaps they can offer you valuable tips and advice on your writing style.
- **Find yourself a fundraising buddy**. Find someone else who is writing fundraising applications. Agree to read and comment on their applications if they do the same for yours. They should know little or nothing about your work, because most donors are in the same position. Ask them to tell you which bits they don't understand, what you have left out and whether they think you have made a good case.

Eh?

Pseuds Corner in *Private Eye* usually provides an object lesson in how not to write. For example:

'The folk/fairytale Cinderella has a four thousand year old history and indicates a paradigm that predates the rise of the fairytale and psychoanalysis. Patterns of a hypnogogic flow or destructuring and a hypnopompic flow or restructuring indicate the capacity to symbolise. Some aspects of projective identification act as a defence whereas anticipatory identification permits a prospective element. Symbol formation contains both regressive and progressive components which are essential for learning and growth.'

Twelve tips for better writing

- write in **shorter sentences**
- **break up longer sentences** into a number of sentences
- **vary the length** of sentences to avoid monotony
- use **shorter rather than longer words**
- **avoid jargon**
- **avoid unsubstantiated superlatives**
- keep it **short and simple**, but make sure you say all you need
- make it **clear and logical**
- improve the **visual appearance** and readability by using shorter paragraphs, headings and sub-heads, indented tables and bullet points rather than continuous prose
- **write for the reader**, with an understanding of their level of knowledge and their perception of the problem
- **avoid** the use of words or concepts which will be controversial or inflammatory. Talk in a common language and build bridges from where you are to where they are
- **avoid patronising** either the donor or the beneficiaries.

Using different media

You can produce your application in whatever form you want. However, be aware of the following.

- **Hand-written letters:** generally only do this if it is a short covering letter to someone you know. Even then, make sure it is neat and in black ink. Assume it is going to be photocopied.
- **Typed:** you want the letter to appear personalised. This doesn't mean the content has to be different in every letter you write. However, each letter should have the person's name and address typed on it and you should usually hand write 'Dear ...' and sign the letter yourself with your name typed underneath. (Obviously it is different if you are writing to 10,000 members.)
- **Print quality:** try to ensure that the letter looks well-produced.
- **Fax/e-mail:** a few donors are happy to receive applications this way. Most aren't. Only do it if the guide books or the funder themselves give this as an option.
- **Cassettes/videos:** these are usually best offered rather than sent. Few funders are so committed to their work that they want to listen to your appeal on the way home or watch it in the evening. If they are, they can always contact you for a copy. Also, you cannot photocopy tapes and videos for the trustees.

  The point at which videos especially come into their own is when you are making a presentation to a company for a major sponsorship, or to an audience of potential donors. In the latter case, you will need back-up literature for people to take away or pledge forms to be signed there and then.

- **Telephone:** telephone sales techniques applied to appeals are being used more and more, especially if there is an obvious case for telephoning. This could work for alumnis, membership and other constituency appeals where people expect to be asked to give, or if there is an extremely urgent reason to give NOW (e.g. disaster appeals).

For example, when the Royal Exchange Theatre was damaged by an IRA bomb in Manchester, the theatre's fundraisers quickly wrote to and then rang round all those on their mailing list to get the money in to start to the re-building process.

The telephone can also be used to follow up a written approach. A major disability charity was hosting a prestigious gala dinner at which it wished to sell tables to company executives. The organiser rang her target list of companies, explained what was going on and asked if she could fax details there and then. She rang back a short time later to see what more information the company needed, but most just agreed there and then. All the tables were booked up within two days.

However, cold-calling grant-making trusts is not a good idea. They want written applications.

6 Writing a Good Application

Donor research

Before you can write a good application, you need to know who you are writing to and what they are interested in. The perfect application to the wrong person will not get the money. An application is a communication from you (who needs the money) to the donor (who has the money). It will only be effective as a communication if it recognises their particular interests and concerns.

So the first thing to do is to find out as much as possible about the donor. Information is relatively easy to come by – from grants guides, from literature produced by the funding sources (most of the larger trusts and the major companies publish reports or produce information for applicants; read this carefully and read between the lines too), from personal contact at meetings and conferences, from gossip 'on the grapevine'. If there's a specific question you need answering, you can always telephone. So try to find out:

- **Who** is the person who will be dealing with your application? This is the Correspondent, who you will be writing to. Their job is to progress the application through the decision-making system, seeking professional or technical advice if necessary – and they may reject the application immediately as being of little relevance or interest to them. Make sure you have their name and job title correct, and that you understand their approach and attitudes. Avoid the application looking like a circular (at all costs). As John Naylor says in the next chapter, applications which look like circulars, however well designed, are rejected straight away.

- **Which budget** is the money coming from? This particularly applies to companies. If you are asking for a donation, this will come from the donations budget and you will need to write to the manager of the charitable donations. If you are proposing a formal sponsorship, this may come from the marketing budget, so you will be writing to the head of marketing. This can also apply to other funders. Some trusts, for example, fund UK-wide but have preferences for certain local areas and allocate some of their annual budget accordingly. If you operate in one of these local areas, stress the importance of your project to local people and show how it is integrated into the local community. Avoid the impression that you are really a national or regional project which happens to be based in that local area.

Fundraising is about building a partnership between two organisations who share the same objectives.

The partnership operates by you doing the work and the funder giving the financial support. So you are not begging for money; you are trying to engage someone with your work.

- What can you learn from policies, priorities and guidelines for applicants? What are they really interested in supporting? Are there particular exclusions, types of project or expenditure which the fund will not support in any circumstances?

- **What grants** have they made previously, and for what sorts of purposes? Can you learn anything from this? For example, do they favour classical arts or community arts? Do they give a higher priority to promoting artistic excellence or involving new people in arts activities? Do they want to bring new audiences to the arts and, if so, do they require you to offer full disabled access to your premises?

- **Are they conventional or radical** in approach? Do they appear to play safe or to take risks? Do they support campaigns? Does any of this have implications for the way in which you describe yourselves? For example, grant-making trusts are often seen as the risk takers, the ones who will push back the boundaries of current provision by funding new approaches to old needs. Very few of them, however, report the failure to deliver of many of the projects they fund. This implies that they are mainly funding projects which are more or less certain to bring in the predicted results. You need to reassure such funders that your project is one of those that will bring in results, even if it is pioneering and innovative.

- What is their grant range? What is a typical grant for a project similar to your own? Are you applying for an amount they can realistically give? For example, a grant-making trust with an income of over £10 million does not want to give its money away in grants of £100; that would be an administrative nightmare. Its usual minimum grant will be about £500. However, for a local trust with an income of £20,000, £500 would be quite a large grant. £500 for a small local company would be a massive grant.

- **Are there any connections** between you and them? Either a personal link, or because there are particular reasons why they should be interested in the cause. These connections may be apparent, or may require some research. For example, a fundraiser for a veterinary faculty discovered that a trustee of a grant-making trust was a former graduate of the university to which she was attached. The trustee had also studied veterinary science. Surprisingly, the trustee was promptly invited to dinner. The grant came through soon after the dinner.

  Similarly, you should always make a connection between you and the company you are writing to. Do you have a personal link (a member of the company staff volunteers for your organisation, the chair of your management committee is the company managing director's bridge partner), a geographical link (you and the company operate in the same area and your users are their customers) or a product link? If you can't create a link, don't bother writing to that company.

- **What is the applications procedure?** In particular, how should applications be presented and when are the deadlines for receipt?

Benefits to the donor

Another aspect of donor research is establishing whether the donor might expect something in return for making the grant.

In this context it is particularly important to understand the difference between sponsorship and a donation.

Sponsorship provides a direct benefit to the donor, which is the prime reason for giving support in the first place. Direct benefits include promotion and publicity, entertainment facilities and other services of commercial benefit to the sponsor.

With a donation, a donor should not normally require any significant direct benefit. Rather they should support the project because they believe it to be socially valuable. But it is important to be aware of some ways in which a donation can bring an indirect benefit to the donor. This can affect the way in which the proposal is presented. For example, the project might do the following.

- **Provide publicity** for the donation and/or identify the donor closely with the project supported. Both of these provide recognition for the donor's contribution. This is especially important to companies and the National Lottery distribution boards. It is also attractive to grant-making trusts if, for example, you will write up the results of the project and disseminate them. The trust is then seen as funding pioneering work and promoting best practice.

- **Deal with a problem that the donor is also concerned with.** This enables the donor to achieve something without actually having to do anything (except give money).

- **Provide a better or cheaper service.** The donor feels they are getting a good return on their money. On the basis that they have a grants budget which has to be spent, you are enabling them to spend their money more cost-effectively.

Presenting your work to funders – four golden rules

---

1. You cannot tell them everything. There isn't time and they wouldn't listen.

2. So you have to select the points that donor is going to be most interested in.

3. In general, don't ask funders to support your organisation.

4. Rather, ask them to support the people you help or the work you do.

It is most important that you offer companies a benefit from their donation, whether it be better staff relations (if they support their employees' voluntary activity), a better name in the community (but show how are you going to achieve this), a good night out for staff, or whatever.

Irrespective of the level of benefit offered to or expected or required by the donor, there are some things you should do with all donors:

■ thank them often and profusely

■ **report back** regularly, showing them all the good things their donation has achieved

■ invite them to open days and events

■ **introduce them** to your patron, VIPs, users etc.

This is not only good manners and an investment in a possible future grant, it also gives them a warm glow of satisfaction and a feeling of involvement.

A step-by-step guide to a well-constructed application

There are no golden rules for writing a proposal. It is very much a matter of personal style and temperament. What works for one person will not necessarily work for another. And what works for you is what you should pay attention to. You may be able to get away with a piece of rhetoric or an impassioned plea for funds in your own handwriting, or only a very brief statement of your plans.

The suggestions that follow are meant as guidelines only. You can reject all of the ideas or pick up on those that seem useful to you. What is important is that you should write an application that you are happy with, that does justice to the work of your organisation and you feel is the best way to persuade someone to support you.

The form of the application

Applications take several forms.

■ **An application form supplied by the donor.** This will tell you precisely what information to supply. Use this format when required to do so. You might also wish to attach a covering letter or supporting information, although your case is likely to be judged on what you have put in the form.

Some application forms are extremely detailed. The National Lottery Charities Board's form, for example, goes on for over 20 pages. Just because you are filling out a form doesn't mean that you switch off your fundraising brain. Try to communicate the important needs you are meeting, your effectiveness in meeting them and the cost-effectiveness of your approach.

■ **An application letter** in which you set out your case and attach supporting information as required. This format will be appropriate in most circumstances and is covered in detail in this chapter.

■ An application and covering letter, together with supporting information. This follows on from the above. Dividing the application letter into two parts, a project proposal and a letter, has certain advantages. The letter can contain the personal information – previous contact with the donor, particular reasons why the donor might be interested, as well as a brief project summary. The project proposal will be more formal and factual; the letter more up-beat, selling the idea of support. This format is especially useful for longer applications or where you are sending a standard proposal to a large number of donors.

The information you supply will then be assessed by the grants secretary, trust director, corporate affairs manager (or whoever) and put forward as a summary and recommendation to the grants committee or trustees, who will make the decision. This is the most usual procedure for all but the smallest grant sources. So, your letter and other beautifully constructed prose may well not be read by the people making the final decisions. All they may see is a summary of your proposal. Therefore, you must make a good, clear case which can be easily understood and summarised.

The structure of the application

Whatever form of proposal you actually produce, it has to fulfil certain functions. It has to inform the reader of who you are and what you intend to do, and it also has to say how much money you need and what you intend to spend it on. It should do this in a clear and logical way. Some of the elements you might use in constructing your proposal are detailed below:

1. The title

It is often a good idea to give your proposal a title, particularly if you can do this in a catchy phrase which captures the essence of what you want to do.

> **A suggested structure for an application letter**
>
> Project title
> Proposal summary
> Introduction: who you are
> The problem or need
> What you will do
> How you will do it
> How much you need to do it
> How you will get the money
> The request
> Why the donor might be interested
> Where the money will come from in the future
> Signing off

2. A summary

For a longer proposal, a summary can be very important. It presents the essence of what the proposal is about, and allows the reader to determine whether it is likely to be of interest. The summary may be presented as a covering letter, or the first paragraph of the application letter itself. It should be clear, concise and specific. It should describe who you are, the scope of your project, and the projected cost. The summary is the first part of your proposal that will be read, and it may be the last! Make sure that you follow the normal fundraising rules, even in the summary paragraph. Be positive and upbeat and state that something really good will happen as a result of this project.

3. The introduction: who you are

Key question

Who are this lot and can I trust them?

This is the section of a proposal where you say who you are. Many proposals tell little or nothing about the applicant organisation and speak only about the project or programme to be conducted. If you are a nationally known organisation, you can state who you are in a line or a sentence. Usually you need to provide more information than this. More often than not proposals are funded on the basis of the reputation of the applicant organisation and its key people, as well as on the basis of the proposed project. The introduction is the section in which you build your credibility as an organisation which deserves to be supported.

Listed below are some of the things you can say about your organisation in your introductory session.

- What **connection** with the funding source you have had in the past. Whether you have had a grant before, or applied and been turned down.
- Your organisation's **goals or objectives** and the basic thrust of your work.
- How you **got started**.
- **How long** you have been around.
- **Anything unique** about the way you got started, or the fact that you pioneered a new type of activity.
- Some of your **most significant accomplishments** as an organisation, or, if you are a new organisation, some of the significant accomplishments of your staff in their previous roles.
- What **support you have received** from other organisations and prominent individuals (accompanied perhaps by letters of endorsement which can be put in an appendix).

You are not putting down history for the sake of history, rather to build your credibility. You are trying to show that you are a safe pair of hands, that you are (hopefully) an imaginative and exciting organisation to be associated with, and that you will continue to deliver a high quality of service.

4. The problem statement or assessment of need: why something needs to be done

In the introduction you have said who you are. Now you will home in on the specific problems that you want to solve through the project you are proposing.

Applicants often make the mistake of painting too broad a picture of all the ills plaguing people, the community or the world. They do not narrow down to a specific problem or problems that are solvable. They give the impression that it will take a hundred times the requested budget even to begin to deal with the problems that have been identified. This is overkill. You may need to confine your definition of the problem so as to allow you to propose a solution. You are then showing how you will make a positive impact within a reasonable amount of time and with reasonable resources.

Another common problem is that applicants bang on about themselves and their needs. 'The community centre roof is falling in so please help us put a new one on.' 'Our play equipment is all broken and our subs don't cover the replacement cost.' 'Our staff are overworked.' Although these may be the real reasons why you are fundraising, always present your proposals on the basis of your users, their needs, their hopes and aspirations.

Document the problem. How do you know that a problem really exists? Don't just assume that everybody knows this is a problem. Use your own or other people's information to strengthen your case. For example, which of the following do you think is more convincing:

- 'It stands to reason that children whose parents cannot read or write will do badly at school'
- 'A recent Joseph Rowntree Foundation report on growing up with parents who have learning difficulties showed conclusively that "children's destinies are not fixed by having a mother or father with learning difficulties". The report went onto argue that...'

Assume that the funder is intensely sceptical about the need for your project. What can you do to prove them wrong? (The National Lottery Charities Board certainly will want hard evidence of the need for your project – bland assertions and generalised statements will not get past them.)

Notwithstanding the above, don't go overboard and fill your proposal with tables, charts and graphs. These will interfere with the flow of the argument. Figures are only helpful if they support an argument being made. If you must use extensive statistics, put them in an appendix, but pull out the key figures for your statement of the problem.

Key question
Who are their users and what is their (the users') problem?

65

When explaining why something needs to be done now you need to do the following:

- Make a **logical connection** between your organisation's background and the problems and needs with which you propose to work.
- Support the existence of the problem by **evidence**. Statistics are one type of evidence. You may also get advice from groups in your community concerned about the problem, from prospective clients, from other organisations working in your community and from professionals in the field.
- Define clearly **the problems** with which you intend to work.
- Make sure that what you want to do is **workable**, that it can be done within a reasonable time, by you, and with a reasonable amount of money.
- Show how something must be done now. If you can't give the application a **sense of urgency**, the funder will turn to one of the many which can.

5. Your objectives: what you intend to do about the problem

Clearly if you have defined a problem then your proposals should offer some relief to the problem. Try to set yourselves objectives for what you propose to do (an objective is a specific, measurable outcome of your project).

If the problem which you identify is a high incidence of vandalism by young people in your community (substantiated, of course), then an objective of your programme should be the reduction of the incidence of vandalism among the youth in your community. If the problem is long-term unemployment, then an objective is getting the long-term unemployed into jobs.

Distinguish between objectives (what you hope to achieve) and methods (how you will do it – *see below*). If you are having difficulty in defining your objectives, try projecting your organisation a year or two into the future. What differences would you hope to see between then and now? What changes will have occurred? These changed dimensions may be the objectives of your programme.

It is worth examining your objectives in a little more detail. Some programmes may create very temporary jobs for people and attract those who are best able to find work by themselves. Even if they reduce the unemployment problem in the short term, after a year or two the problem will be back, as bad or worse than ever. You should be concerned about the quality of your work as well as the quantity (which is just the number of people you are helping).

Be as precise as you can in describing who you are helping and the severity of the problems being tackled, the extent of the service being provided, and the impact on those you are helping.

Key question

What do they want to do to make life better for their users?

For example:

'In 40% of the households in XXX area there is no wage earner. Attendance on training and further education courses is Y% lower than the national average. The majority of these families are locked into a cycle of debt and dependence on benefits (Z% of households have had no private income coming into the home for over two years).

'Our pilot project showed how we can help people break out of this cycle. As a result of the XXX Initiative, P% of those attending were still in training or education after six months and Q% had already found full or part-time work. As a result, their household income has risen by R%. More importantly, they now feel the have control over their own lives and futures.'

You can take it further to demonstrate the cost-effectiveness and value for money your project represents. Many grant-makers are now judging applications on the impact or outcome of the work and the value for the money they are putting up.

Try to set specific targets for the project (the National Lottery Charities Board will require this anyway). On the above example you could say something like: 'By the end of the three-year project, we expect a further W people to have gone through our X programme. Of these, Y will then go onto formal job training or into further education and Z will be in full or part-time work.' This will give you a clear basis to measure the success of your work and reassure the funder that the project is well planned and thought through.

6. The methods: how you will attempt to do it

You have already stated who you are, the problem you want to work with, your objectives (which promise a solution to or reduction of the problem). Now you are going to explain how you intend to bring about these results.

You will need to describe the methods you will use and the activities you will conduct to accomplish your objectives. You will also need to persuade the funder that they will work. You can do this by demonstrating that:

Key question
How do I know that it will work?

- this project is **based on a successful model** developed elsewhere;
- it is a **natural extension** of work you have already undertaken, so it is not some great leap in the dark;
- you have **experienced and well-qualified people** to run the project;
- you have the **support and commitment of the users**, and that they have been involved in the project's planning;
- it has the **backing of key people and agencies**, which can act as a kind of independent verification of the project plan;
- it is **clearly thought through** with clear targets and review processes at regular intervals;

- the work you have done in the past gives confidence that this new project is **well within your capabilities**.

The informed donor may want to know why you have selected these methods, particularly for an innovative project. This requires you to know a good deal about other projects of a similar nature. Who else is working on the problem and where? What methods have been tried in the past, and what are being tried now, and with what results? In other words, can you justify or substantiate your approach?

7. The budget: how much you will need to do this work

Fundraising is really about selling an idea rather than asking for money. However, once you have sold the idea to someone with the means and inclination to support you, you then need to get down to the business of asking for money.

The budget is simply a statement of what you intend to spend on the project. It will include the direct project expenditure and possibly also an allocation of overhead costs. In the application you may want to give a total budget figure or you might break it down into smaller items according to what you think the particular donor is interested in (e.g. a particular project, idea or piece of equipment). Either way, the budget should show how the whole thing fits together. See Chapter 4 Costing a Project for more information.

If you are applying for a grant over several years, inflation can pose a problem. There are two ways of tackling this. Firstly, you can allow for inflation at a guessed rate; secondly you can compute your own budget at present costs and ask for an inflation allowance to be added each year according to the prevailing level. If you are in doubt, consult the funder as they may have specific ways of dealing with this.

8. Funding plan

If you are only applying to a donor for part of the money you need, explain where you intend to obtain the balance. The funder will be asking two key questions:

- **What is their track record in fundraising?** What does this tell me about their ability to get money for this project? For example, if you have raised around £50,000 a year from grant-making trusts for the last six years and you are currently asking for a £30,000 project, the trust you are writing to will be pretty confident in your ability to raise the full amount and will contribute accordingly. If you have never raised a penny from trusts and now expect to get £100,000 over the next year, this looks like wishful thinking unless you can make a convincing case otherwise.

Key question

How much is it going to cost?

Key question

Where are they getting the money from?

- **Who else has put money in?** The more money you have raised or had promised from elsewhere, the more confidence this funder will have in your ability to get the project fully funded.

If you are applying for a piece of equipment or a capital project, it's not just a matter of showing how you can raise the money to buy the equipment. You must also demonstrate that you have the resources to use it. Donors don't like paying for a building or an expensive piece of equipment only to find it lying idle as you can't afford to use it. You need to demonstrate how you intend to meet these running costs.

9. The request: how much to ask for

At this stage, many applications tail off into a murmur that any contribution would be gratefully received. This is partly due to an embarrassment about asking for money. It is also untrue as you would be angry and insulted if the funder sent back just £1!

But going back to first principles, fundraising is about making a good case, selling a cause. Once the case is made and the importance of the project is accepted by the donor, making a grant is something that is done willingly because the donor wants to help.

The only question is how much to give. Here it can be helpful to the donor if you make a specific request rather than ask them to decide what is appropriate. Of course, before you do this you need to know how much the donor is able to give – the total amount they have to give and a typical size of grant made in the past to similar organisations for similar purposes. Then you can assess the likely grant range which this donor might consider and ask for a specific amount. You can make this suggestion in a number of ways:

- **ask directly for a specific sum** (£5,000, or £2,500 for three years)
- **state that you need to raise a specific sum** which you hope to get from a specified number of donors (£20,000 in six grants) which gives a picture for how much each might contribute
- **provide a shopping list** (£12,000 for the project itself, £3,000 for the research, £3,000 for the publication, £2,000 for the evaluation etc.)
- if you have already received grants, then **state how much has been committed** and from what sources. This gives an opportunity for the donor to peg the grant accordingly.

The other thing you need to do is show thefunder how their grant fits into the overall picture. So you need to say how much you need in total, where it is coming from and what you expect that donor to give. For example: 'We need to raise £210,000. Our members have already committed £60,000 and the health authority has agreed to match this amount. We expect to raise a further £40,000 from fundraising events, £20,000 from local and national companies and £30,000 from grant-making trusts. I am therefore writing to ask you for…'.

10. The rationale: why the donor might be interested

There are many reasons why the donor might be interested in your proposal:

- you are running a **good project** which falls **within their stated policies** and priorities
- you have **already received a grant** from them, and a further grant is an investment in your success
- they have **a known interest** or some particular connection with the problem or cause
- there is a **personal connection** which it will pay to highlight
- there is a **payback** for them in the form of good publicity.

Key question

So why does it apply to us?

Whatever the reason, you may want to mention it in the application (or the covering letter or a conversation with the donor). This is particularly important when you are approaching a company who will be wanting to know what PR or other commercial benefit they will get from their support.

11. Where will the money come from in future?

Another important consideration is what you intend to do when the grant you are seeking runs out. Is your project time-limited, say three years or less? If so, you don't have to worry about getting funding beyond then. However, often you are trying to get a new project going on the basis that if it works you will want it to continue for as long as necessary (and certainly beyond three years). Given that most funders will not give grants for more than three years, what happens when their funding runs out?

Key question

If the project is there for the long term, how are they going to pay for it?

You need to think about this at the outset, as no funding source wants to be locked into supporting a project for ever. One way used to be to get a commitment from a statutory authority to take over the project once it had proved itself; but with cutbacks in public spending, this has become increasingly difficult, if not impossible. So what are the options?

- If the statutory authority will not definitely commit itself to funding the whole project, then they may at least indicate a willingness to consider a funding application if the project proves successful.
- You may be able to show that the project fits in with a statutory service's priorities and that you expect to be able to run it on a contract basis.
- The project may generate an income of its own (e.g. you can build in a charging structure to users or another body which will grow to cover the project's costs within the life span of the grant).

- You are developing your general fundraising or income-generating activities and expect to be able to pay for the project from within your own resources.
- Over the lifetime of the grant you will be aiming to double your membership to bring in an additional £X a year. Some of this can be transferred to paying for the project from year four onwards.

It may well be that you use a combination of the above, or have some other scheme of your own. The key thing to do is think about it now and show the funder that you are planning ahead. You may not be certain that you will be able to obtain funding in the way you suggest, but at least you will have thought about the problem at an early stage and provided some reassurance to those who would like to fund you. Also, it gives you a fundraising plan to be getting on with.

As the National Lottery Charities Board puts it: 'Assure us that your organisation has a sensible plan to secure new sources of funding if the project is expected to continue when our grant has expired'.

12. The signatory: who puts their name to the application

Who signs the letter can be important. If the applicant is recognised or known to the donor, this can be helpful. The following are possible signatories:

- the **project leader**
- the **fundraiser** or development officer
- the organisation's **director**
- the **chair of the trustees** or management committee
- an **appeal patron**
- an **expert** or **prominent personality** with some connection with the cause.

Who is the best person for the job depends very much on the nature of the body you are approaching. It is up to you to decide who will be the best signatory to the application. But beware the points listed below.

- You write saying that you are doing so at the suggestion of a prominent person (connected with you and known to them). This can imply that that person is too busy to be able to or to want to make the application in person.
- Follow up information and contact will be with another person. This again implies that the person signing the letter is too important or too busy to be concerned with following it up. As a general principle any signatory should be prepared, at least, to attend a follow-up meeting with the donor (diary permitting) to discuss the grant.

Key points

The main points to remember in any application are:

- build the credibility of your organisation

- support the need for your proposed project

- develop clear, specific, measurable and attainable objectives

- justify your approach

- include methods for evaluating your progress

- show how your future funding will go

- use simple, clear, understandable language – avoid jargon and rhetoric

- say it concisely and briefly

- prepare a realistic budget and include all relevant costs.

The ingredients of a good application – a summary

The application should be addressed to a named individual at the funding body. It could contain all of the following:

- **Proposal title**, a catchy phrase encapsulating the essence of what you propose to do.

- **Proposal summary** (or covering letter) for a longer application highlighting the key points.

- **Introduction** explaining who you are, what you do and why you're wonderful.

- **Problem statement** or assessment of need, showing why something needs to be done now.

- **Project objectives** explaining what you intend to do and the outcome you expect.

- **Method** describing how you intend to set about undertaking the project.

- **Budget** showing the resources you need to carry out the work.

- **Funding plan** showing how you intend to set about raising the money.

- **Request** asking the donor to make a contribution (of a specified amount)

- **Rationale for the donation** stating why you believe it appropriate for the donor to say yes. This could be included in the covering letter.

- **The longer term**, saying where the money will come from in the future (if you want the project to continue) and what else you expect to come out of the project.

- **Signing off** mentioning the information you are attaching to the application, and suggesting who to contact for further information or to arrange a project visit. Who signs the letter can also be important.

- **Back up information** to support your application.

- The signatory has a job title which appears too junior – fundraising assistant or assistant to the director, for example. Again, this implies that you are not treating the application seriously. If you are given the responsibility for signing the letter and your job title is inadequate, then get promoted – or at least get it agreed that you can use a more appropriate job title when signing fundraising letters.
- The signatory is a fundraising consultant acting on your behalf. There are two problems here:

  (i) the consultant will almost certainly become a Professional Fundraiser under the terms of the 1993 Charities Act and will have to make some rather clumsy-looking declarations about how they are being paid for their work.

  (ii) many funders refuse to consider appeals from a third party on behalf of a charity. Even if they don't rule you out on these grounds, donors respond best to direct requests, even though the approach has been put together with professional advice.

Length of the application

You cannot tell funders everything. You haven't got time and they won't read it. You just need to tell them enough. It is difficult enough reading thirty applications each day, every day – which is what many donors have to do. Put yourself in their position. You would pick up an application, look at who it was from, read the first paragraph and then possibly decide that the application was really worth bothering with. If you did read all of it, you may skip through much of the text simply because there was so much to read.

On the other hand, if it was clear, to the point and brief it would be so much easier to absorb the information. Funders are not paying you for the words you write. So you don't have to provide a lot of words to get a lot of money. Nor is it a case of 'never mind the quality, feel the width'. You have to show what you are doing, give evidence that it is an exciting project that meets a real and important need, and that you can make an impact.

- Try to keep the application to one page, whether writing to a trust or a company. This means that it can be easily photocopied and stands less chance of being summarised and possibly misrepresented by someone else. Obviously, for a very major project you might want to go into more detail, but here you can write a much shorter summary proposal.
- If in doubt, leave it out. Each point must add something to the case you are making. If it doesn't, it is making a negative impact by obscuring those parts of the application that do.
- You can always supply more detail in an attachment, although this may not be read. Or you can indicate that further information is

available on request, which they will seldom ask for. Or they will ask to meet you; any discussion will generate far more useful and revealing information about the proposal and your competence than anything you put in writing.

A good application is one that 'shouts out' from the pile to be read. It communicates effectively and efficiently all that is needed for the reader to come to a sensible decision on what to do with it.

Back up information

You might want to include any or all of these:

- Your organisation's **annual report and accounts**, or a leaflet containing the information in an abridged form (this would include photographs of your work wherever possible).
- A **detailed budget** for the project.
- A **detailed plan** for the project.
- **Visual material**, such as photographs of the project in action or architectural drawings for a building project.
- A **background briefing** on the need for the project (to include key statistics which bolster your case).
- A **case study** or several examples of the problem or what you can achieve.
- A **list of donors** and contributors.
- A **fundraising plan** (where and who you intend to get the money from).
- **Curriculum vitae** of the key personnel involved in the project.
- A **list of trustees**, patrons, vice-presidents or other key supporters.
- **Letters of endorsement** from prominent people/other funders/ users/ beneficiaries.
- A **quotes sheet** where users, community leaders and other notables say really positive things about you.
- Photocopies of **press cuttings**.

Don't rely on the attachments. Assume the only things the funder reads are the letter and budget. They should have a full understanding of who you are, what you want to do, why it's important and what it will cost. If you keep writing in the letter 'For further information see attached', they probably won't.

Always attach a budget for the project, an annual report and set of accounts. Over and above that, think what the donors will want to know, and what they will need to know before they give their support. Don't overload the system by sending everything. This is a waste of money, a waste of paper, and it will cost more to post. Also, they won't all be photocopied for the trustees or grants committee members.

Finally, all attachments are fundraising documents. The same rules which apply to writing your fundraising letter apply to the attachments (short sentences, easy to read, lots of sub headings etc.). If they are not easy to read or are packed with jargon, either re-write them or leave them out.

What to do with your application

You need to think about and plan how, when and to whom to send off your application. You may have targeted a number of potentially interested sources and need several grants to make up the total cost of the project. Who should you approach first? And for how much? How can you maximise your chances of meeting your fundraising target? And how can you make sure that you raise the money you need within often tight deadlines?

There are no specific answers to these questions. It is as much a matter of your temperament and style as anything else. But the following points may help.

1. Apply immediately

Applications for small sums to the smaller trusts can be sent out whenever you like. Many of these trusts meet infrequently (often only once a year), and it may be some time before you hear the outcomes of your appeal. So the sooner you get these applications out, the better.

However, small local grants can be very useful in levering out large national ones. The fact of the endorsement is probably more useful to you than the amount of money they give, as it gives confidence to the national trust that those on the ground know, like and trust you. But remember the national trust will only know you have got local money if you tell them!

2. The blanket approach

Suppose you have identified 30 sources as being potentially interested in your work; you might then send out all 30 applications at once. The advantage of this is that you will have actually asked 30 people to support you; and they can then decide whether to do so or not. The disadvantage is that your appeal may not be as strong as where you adopt the step-by-step approach (*discussed below*).

In your application, you might state that you are approaching a number of sources, and even name some of them. You might try to indicate in some way how much you would like each to give (e.g. 'We are writing to you and eight other major trusts asking for a total of £30,000' – *for more information, see pp 69–70*).

Some donors will not reply. Some will acknowledge receipt of your application, and that will be the last you hear. Some will want further information. A few might request a meeting. Some will simply send you a cheque, if your application is successful.

You can use their response to improve your chances. If one of your top prospects says 'no', it may be worth politely finding out why, possibly asking for a meeting or a visit so that you an explain the importance of your work in greater depth. There are many instances of an applicant being able to turn a 'no' into a 'yes' in this way. In any case, you will begin to accumulate information about their approach to grant-making which will improve your chances of success next time around.

If you have been successful, you can send a follow-up letter to some of the other trusts that have not yet reached a decision, outlining the progress of the appeal. This can remind them that your appeal is outstanding, as well as give them further information which might enhance your chances.

If you fall just short of your target, don't just keep trying to find yet another untapped source of money. Go back and ask a few of your key supporters if there is the possibility of topping up their support with a further small grant.

Fundraising is not 'fair'. The more you raise, the easier it is to raise more. Therefore, trumpet your success to funders, especially those who have not yet decided whether to give you a grant.

3. The step-by-step approach

Here you identify from your list of potential sources a few which you believe are more likely to be interested in you and which have the resources to make a substantial grant. If you are applying for a large grant from a statutory source, it is always important to do this first, and to get some commitment before approaching others for support. The statutory grant can be the key component in your fundraising plan, and other donors may want to be assured that you have got what you can out of statutory rather than charitable funds.

How you approach your major donors will depend on their application procedures, how well you are known to them and whether they have supported you previously. You may be able to arrange a meeting to discuss your proposal; you may want to find out first about the grant cycle, when applications are due in and when they will be considered.

Do all you can to get your large grants committed. Once you have got your first grant, everything then becomes much easier. Your target is reduced; you have an endorsement for what you are doing; and your confidence grows. This makes it more likely that others will agree to support you.

For each approach, mention something of your fundraising strategy. Ask for support at a specific level and put this into the context of your overall fundraising plans for the project. Tell them who has already supported you. Tell them who else you are approaching. Suggest to them that their 'lead' grant might encourage others to give to you. In other words, you will be able to write: 'We need a total of £30,000 from grant-making trusts. The XXX Foundation has already given a grant of £8,000, so now we only need a further £22,000. Therefore, I am writing to you and eight other major trusts asking for a total of £22,000.' (In fundraising, you always quote the highest figure you need, showing how much has been raised and how much you still need.)

4. The delayed approach

In most applications, you will be asking for money. But there are other possibilities. You can send an outline of your proposals and ask for a meeting to discuss your ideas. This would only be worthwhile where you are already well-known to the donor (*see Example 3 in Chapter 7*). Otherwise, they normally prefer a full written proposal in the first instance.

You can try to get them to visit you. Open days, launches and other events can provide suitable opportunities for this. If you are organising a prestigious event, this can be a particularly appropriate time to get potential supporters to visit you. Some projects, such as City Farms, have a product which is inherently attractive to donors, and experience shows that most of the people who visit eventually decide to give financial support. In such circumstances, the challenge is to find ways of getting them to accept an invitation to visit you.

You can try to get yourself known in the grant-making world before you actually apply. This means:

- meeting grants administrators at events and conferences, and making sure you introduce yourself
- sending out your annual report (for information purposes only) to potential supporters
- seeking and getting publicity in the media
- building your trustee, patron or supporter base so that you create wider contacts for your organisation.

It is extremely hard to obtain substantial support for a project when you have never received support before. This may mean presenting more modest needs now, and building on this over time. It also means being very clear about which funders you are targeting over the next five years or so and making sure you think strategically about how you will do this.

What to do after the application

Mostly you will do nothing, except wait for a response. You can chase up your letter with a phone call to find out if it has arrived, when it will be considered, and whether they require any further information.

This, at least, has the advantage of putting a human voice to a written application. But you do need to do this carefully. There is a danger of appearing to hassle them, which they will resent.

When you do receive a positive reply, say 'thank you' immediately. Put the donor on a mailing list to receive information on your work (such as annual reports and copies of the publications you produce). Note any conditions of the grant that have to be met (terms for spending the money, reporting and audit requirements, etc.).

Keep a card index of your contacts. Add information from your refusals as well as your successes. They may give reasons for turning you down. Note these, as this can help you next time, although what they say may be out of politeness rather than the bare truth. When you do re-apply, remind them that you have applied before. Remember that the bodies that have supported you this time are quite likely to want to support you again (unless they have a specific policy of not doing so).

You should consider when and how next to approach them. As most grant-making bodies work on annual grant cycles, you may decide to go back for more support next year. As a rule, never apply to the same funder more than once in their financial year.

Anybody who has turned you down should be seen as a possibility for future support (unless there are clear reasons why they will never support you). You have decided that they are likely to be interested. The only problem is that they have not yet come to the same conclusion. It is your challenge to present a better case next time or even the time after. Persistence can pay.

A first application should be seen as the beginning, not the end, of the process. Success in raising money depends as much on building relationships and not giving up, as on writing a good application for a good project.

Timing and timescale

One reason many applications fail is that they are made too late. The time to think about applying is well before you need the money. This means that planning ahead is vital. Raising money to extricate yourself from a financial crisis is by far the most difficult form of fundraising.

There are various stages in the application process, each with a time scale attached:

- **getting known** and getting to know potential supporters
- **building credibility** with a donor, so that they will be happy to give you a real grant rather than a token donation

Fundraising takes time. The more time you leave the better. Try to plan at least a year ahead.

And when you receive a grant, think of this as the first of many instalments, not the one and only. Put time and energy into building the relationship.

- **developing your fundraising ideas** and completing a written application. This might include a process of discussion with potential donors
- **submitting a formal application**
- **assessing the application** and making a recommendation to the trustees or grants committee
- the **timescale for their decision** at a trustee or grants committee meeting
- **communication of the decision** to the applicant, which may require an acceptance by the applicant of the terms and conditions of the grant before the money can be paid over.

The first two stages can take many years, but time spent on building credibility is never wasted. The subsequent phases also take time. The trustees or grants committee may only meet quarterly and may require applications to be submitted at least one month in advance. The grants budget at the next trustee meeting may already be fully absorbed, and the applicant might only stand any real chance if the application is deferred until a subsequent meeting.

Organisations in receipt of local authority funding must apply in the late Summer for grants for the year beginning the following May. And they may be wise to start preliminary discussions for the next year's grant at about the time that the current year's grant is confirmed.

Of course, there will always be emergencies or projects where the need was unforeseen which need to be funded immediately. The point here is that if you have already developed good relationships with potential funders, securing emergency funding is that much easier. Conversely, if you haven't done the preparatory work it is difficult and often impossible to get funded at short notice, however desperate the need.

7 The Funder's Viewpoint

This chapter has been written by John Naylor, Secretary and Treasurer of the Carnegie United Kingdom Trust. The Trust is widely respected as one of the most pioneering and thoughtful UK grant-making bodies. Here John explains how his trustees judge applications. His comments show:

- the importance of understanding who you are writing to and exactly what they are interested in
- that the applications business can be a fairly long and involved process. This is where the detailed preparation work outlined earlier in this book comes into its own
- that although the Carnegie Trust is mainly interested in the quality of the idea rather than the excellence of the application letter, a clearly thought through and well-presented case gives you a much greater chance of success. For example, the second case study nearly failed to get a grant partly because the Trust was not sure of their capacity to deliver (their credibility).

A word of warning: not all funders have the resources to undertake such in-depth analyses of interesting applications. Although many major trusts operate on this basis, most companies will accept or reject appeals on sight (so the approach in *Example 3* is unlikely to succeed), but will be more prepared to go with people they know (the personal contact in *Example 1* may well have worked in their case). Again, be sure of what kind of donor you are writing to and how they operate.

John Naylor writes:
In judging an application, the Carnegie United Kingdom Trust uses three main criteria.

1. Is it within our guidelines?

Every five years, the Trust reviews its grant-giving policies and identifies priorities, some of which may be changed, for the next five years. With limited funds and huge demands, this ensures:

- funds are focused and can potentially make an impact
- expertise for judging applications is available where necessary
- processing of short-listed applications is manageable.

Example 1 shows how, even if powerfully supported, an application outside the guidelines will be rejected (the Carnegie UK Trust is particularly rigorous on this).

2. What is the quality of the idea?

Sometimes an excellent idea can be disguised by an inadequate application. *Example 2* shows how a good idea – which was nearly rejected by trustees – eventually played an important part in shaping Trust policies.

Example 3 shows how a simple idea was enhanced by taking a wider, more visionary approach and presenting it well. Trust guidelines say: 'Preference is given to proposals which are innovative and developmental; have potential to influence policy and practice more widely; and are undertaken in partnership with others'. Projects need to show how they fit in with this.

3. Can the management deliver?

Most applications are considered purely on their merits. Often we have not met the applicant and so can take no reassurance from prior knowledge. However, a key question for us is whether the project can deliver its aims and objectives. A well-written application inspires confidence in the trustees that the organisation has credibility, the management is capable and the project will achieve its goals. *Example 4* illustrates this.

Example 1

Is it within guidelines?

Nine out of ten applications to the Carnegie UK Trust (and many other trusts) fail to progress beyond initial vetting because they do not fall within the funder's guidelines. An applicant might only need a few thousand pounds to discover a cure for cancer but as the Trust does not currently support medical causes, it would receive automatic rejection.

The Carnegie UK Trust receives and rejects many applications which clearly fall outside its precise guidelines for support. These are typically:

- from individuals, often with heart-rending stories;
- circulars which with the sophistication of IT have become more refined but are nevertheless circulars;
- capital requests, particularly for buildings.

Sometimes applicants clearly think that using the 'right' person and by-passing the staff and normal procedures either alleviates the need

Example 1

Dear Ken

I have recently agreed to become a Vice Patron of the *** Appeal. We have the large sum of £1.5 million to raise within the next eighteen months, this will provide continued and additional help to our members from the W area, who are homeless or deprived.

*** provides free membership to those homeless and deprived who have nowhere else to go. The Centre is situated in *** and is open 7 days a week, 365 days a year, from 9am to 7pm. It offers a wide range of services covering 3 meals a day, a laundry service, a Medical Centre, Counselling and of course a warm and safe place to meet and regain social contact. Enclosed is a Case for Support which fully explains our services as well as the aims and objectives of this Appeal.

When the Club opened in ***, the anticipated membership was around 150 during the first year. We now realise that this was a vast underestimate of the problem, for just over a year and a half later, nearly 3,000 men and women of all ages and races have registered as members, thus our resources are woefully overstretched.

It is because of this vast demand as well as the expected future demand that we have decided to launch this *** Appeal to raise £1.5 million to ensure the current services are maintained and that future projects, such as a Night Shelter can be introduced, which will then provide a 24 hour safe haven for the members.

This Appeal has been structured so as to cover the Club's existing services and future project costs over the next 3 years. From this a new Fund-raising Department will be formed, which will be more than capable of raising the on-going revenue costs needed for future years.

We are aiming to obtain a large percentage of the Appeal target from Lottery funds, but we are also relying heavily on the generosity of the Voluntary Sector. I know that The Carnegie UK Trust generously donates a substantial sum to Charity each year and it would help me enormously if your Trust could consider supporting this Appeal with a substantial donation. A full breakdown of the Appeal target is attached to this application.

I do hope that you will feel, as I do, that this Appeal is worthy of support and that your Trust will be able to assist in containing a major problem which currently exists in our society by providing funds for those who devote themselves to the relief of poverty and homelessness.

I look forward to receiving your support.

We had a word about this on the phone and it would be wonderful if the Carnegie Trust could help.

Yours ever

John

Lord Ponsonby

for proper targeting or will enable the guidelines to be circumvented. (Occasionally, there is a combination of the failure to consider guidelines, the sophisticated circular and the use of the 'right' person!)

Recently, the Trust received three identical applications addressed individually and signed by hand by three titled gentlemen to three different Carnegie UK trustees (including the chairman). Each titled person received a polite rejection after I had consulted individually with each of the three trustees. The request was for funds for a building. Buildings are, however, a specific exclusion for us. Much time and effort was therefore wasted by the applicant and the Trust – time which everyone could have spent more profitably.

Although the example given on p. 83 appears to be a good project it is not a very good application, for the following reasons.

- It doesn't say where the £1.5 million is coming from.
- Nor does it say how the project will be funded long-term (other than a new fundraising department will 'be more than capable of raising the on-going revenue costs needed for future years' – not very convincing).
- It assumes that the Carnegie Trust simply gives money 'to Charity', i.e. to any charity. Like the vast majority of trusts, it does not.
- How much do you think it is expecting Carnegie to give?

Far too much weight is attached to the enclosed 'Case for Support'. You can't assume that the funder will read all the supporting material you send. The letter must make the case for you. By doing this, the application then begs a series of questions:

- Are numbers expected to grow still further? If so, can the project cope?
- Does it have any support from other agencies?
- Do the users like the service they get?
- What happens to the users? Do they go on to permanent housing, education, training, employment, volunteer activities within the project?

Don't say 'but all the answers are in the supporting material'. The funder may not get that far.

Example 2

A good idea that was nearly rejected by the trustees

This application by Raw Material (*see pp. 86–88*)was deferred by our trustees, something that only happens very occasionally. Their criticisms were:

- although the Trust encourages organisations to work together, this

partnership seemed artificial. Raw Material would be better alone
- the projects to be supported by Raw Material did not have clear aims and criteria for success. The application was simply not sufficiently clear
- trustees were not convinced of the quality of Raw Material's work.

The Trustees deferred a decision rather than rejected the proposal for the following reasons.
- Raw Material seemed to be offering relevant artistic experiences to young people post-school (the Trust's policy guideline) and particularly to those who were not usually offered such experiences.
- Multi-media had not been supported by the Trust. Some trustees felt that this would be increasingly significant in the future and therefore ought to be given more consideration. (However, if the Trust had already supported some multi-media projects, this factor would not have been so much in Raw Material's favour – in this sense they struck lucky.)
- On-line support for regional projects was again unusual, could be increasingly common in the future and, it was therefore decided, ought to be considered more closely.
- The Trust Secretary had seen Raw Material in operation and reported positively.

Two trustees were identified to review a revised application.
- The application was simplified to include only Raw Material. The other organisation unfortunately went out of operation.
- A limited number (three instead of six) regional developments were identified as were their aims and outcomes.
- One instead of two-year funding was given as there were still concerns – some of them about the new technology.

However, note the following points.
- Further funding has been given to Raw Material in the light of the success of the first three projects. Fundraising is not all about getting as much as possible now. Getting and spending a small grant well can be the best way of building larger and long-term support, so think strategically about developing a relationship with funders that allows you to go back again and again.
- Multi-media has become a separate section in the Trust's most recent policy guidelines.
- Comedia, in its research on arts multi-media and its social impact, have identified Raw Material as an example of good practice.

Example 2

The following is a rather weak project description rather than letter of application

Raw Material Music and Media and **Youth Adventure**

Joint Application to the Carnegie UK Trust

A national youth development scheme through arts and media technology

Title 'SPEAK OUT'

Rationale
Raw Material and Youth Adventure seek to stimulate and empower young people to create a new agenda for themselves, in recognition of the uncertain futures they face and the risks they confront.

The two organisations do this by giving young people opportunities and motivation
- to express themselves
- to communicate their needs and solutions to their peers and adults
- to explore their diverse cultural backgrounds and the wider world of which they are citizens
- to identify skills in emerging areas of economic activity
- to support their own community however they interpret this.

Raw Material offers resources and expertise in developing arts schemes to aid community development. The project seeks to inspire young people and at the same time help them make positive choices about how they live their lives and pursue career opportunities.

Youth Adventure uses the opportunity for young people to gain a direct grant for cultural, entrepreneurial and developmental activities, such as music making, to motivate young people in individual decision making and practice of skills for life and work and to unlock opportunities for them to build self confidence and community esteem.

Raw Material and *Youth Adventure* have a national remit and yet, being of a modest size, need to develop nationally within a supportive framework.

Both organisations intend to do so by developing a rolling programme of projects spreading out across the country.

Raw Material is already a referrer to YA and is represented on YA's grants committee. YA has in its three year business plans identified six priority target groups and twenty geographical areas to which this project relates.

Media arts, technology, and young people
Despite the important place of media arts technology in contemporary life and in the 'market place', few young people have the opportunities or resources to learn how to use it. There are far fewer opportunities for those living outside central London, who have special needs or who lack confidence and role models.

With rapid developments in information and communications technology, opportunities for education, vocational training and employment are opening up and the domestic market in low cost technology is growing.

Unless these new opportunities are opened up to all sections of society through access and education, a hierarchy of communication will be created with whole sections of society unable to receive or extend information.

The young people who come into contact with Raw Material and Youth Adventure have often already been failed in education and literacy. This project aims to equip them with new incentives and methods of communication; giving them the ability to create new channels of debate, entertainment and expression on the '*information highway*'.

Project elements

1. From November 1994 RM and YA to assemble national contact list of groups across the UK whose members are 16-25, not at school, broadly defined as disadvantaged and known to have an interest in music, performing and creative arts, media, communications and audio visual technology.

This list will include contacts already made by RM and referrals to YA (see example list).

Each group would be approached with the offer of help to establish a training project in music and/or media production.

2. RM would develop a tailored project for each group wishing to participate. This development would involve:

- discussions with the groups staff and users and RM staff and users/young volunteers
- individual young RM users would opt to attach themselves to a specific project in the role of facilitator for the users of the participating group
- the specific content of each project and its format would be developed in liaison with RM and the group (see example list)
- a partnership plan covering the structure of *joint funding* would be agreed. YA would offer the possibility of grants to individual young leaders of participating groups. The availability of *direct grant aid* would have the effect of motivating participation and the self planning of projects by young people.

3. Individual young RM users participating as facilitators would be trained by YA to act as outreach recruitment volunteers while at the group. During their participation they would identify, recruit and train one or more young users of the host group to act as outreach volunteer for YA.

4. Projects would take place over a specified term from January 1995, of either a two week block or several weekly sessions. They would be carried out on site at the participating group, at RM production studios and/or at similar local facility which would be identified in co-operation with the local group and YA.

Each project would consist of a structured course that would enable young people to learn about and use hi-tech music and video production facilities, with expert tutors who are skilled and experienced in work with a wide range of groups (see Raw Material general information pack).

5. Exchanges would be facilitated to enable young people from participating groups to return to RM on work visits, placements and as participants or producers on production projects. Such visits would include top-up outreach training from YA.

6. Outreach volunteering for YA would entail spreading the word about the availability of YA funds, providing advice and information to potential applicants on YA's criteria and acting as

continued overleaf

a link person between YA and its past beneficiaries for volunteer recruitment, monitoring and evaluation purposes. Such representation of YA would provide the embryo of what would then be developed by YA into a local volunteering project.

7. August 1995 – participating groups, having benefited from RM training and facilitation would then set up pilot projects of their own. RM would provide help line/ modem back up. YA would provide possibility of grant aid to individual participants.

8. RM would establish a *bulletin board* using PC, low cost modem and telephone line to network information, advice, job opportunities, news, events, to all participants.

9. October/November 1995 – showcase event, evaluation and report.

The proposal ends with a list of participating projects

Example 3

A simple idea enhanced by taking a wider, more visionary approach

It may be that you are not yet ready to make a formal approach to the funder. You may need to discuss ideas with them first. Here is a project which took its time in making the right application. However, this approach only works if:

- you have the time
- you know the funder in the first place (as the chatty tone of the letters shows)
- you show a clear understanding of the funder's interests and concerns from the outset and don't trade on personal loyalties (see example 1 of the dangers of this)
- you have a sufficiently interesting project to make this worthwhile.

The compelling parts of the application were as follows.
- Parents had to be committed. Instead of straight youth work it moved to parenting.
- Parents and young people had to jointly agree individual development targets. It was not a generalised unfocused approach.
- There was a well-worked and clearly presented project proposal.
- If the programme was successful, there would be a strategy to enable the approach to be used elsewhere in Ireland – a small input from the Trust can potentially create a major impact.
- There was a cross-community dimension which was particularly significant in the Lurgan location where the church was in a Protestant island surrounded by Catholics. (This was pointed out by the Trust's Irish trustee.)

Example 3

Introductory letter

19 April 1993

Dear John,

Greetings from Ireland! I tried to speak to you on the phone before Easter, but I understand you were out of the office for a number of days. I also heard from Stephen Turner that he saw you at your presentation at the National Council Assembly. It is hard to keep pace with all the changes these days.

Since moving to my new post, I have been looking more carefully at the needs of the elderly here in Lurgan. I obtained a copy of the Carnegie Inquiry into the Third Age. I was particularly interested in the findings and have consequently booked in to the Conference on Wednesday 28/Thursday 29 April in London, in order to glean more information. I am enclosing a copy of 'Serve Our Seniors' which is a survey undertaken by Shankill Parish Caring Association at the end of last year. We are now proceeding with the implementation of the recommendations and will also be developing other initiatives for the Third Age Group.

At the other end of the scale we have been taking a particular look at Parenting. We have been quite concerned that the Youth Service, which does an excellent job, is not really hitting at the core of the problem. It is generally felt that we need to be exercising much greater influence on the 5 to 10 age group. It is the view that this can be done most successfully in partnership with parents and other members of the family. To this end the 3 year PACT Project has been developed with a commencement date scheduled for 1 August 1993. In both cases we see our role under Shankill Parish Caring Association which will shortly be registered as a charity, as developing models which can be replicated elsewhere in Northern Ireland and further afield.

I am writing to you now to seek your opinion and advice in presenting one or other or maybe both to the Carnegie Trust under the Community Service Section for support. Perhaps you would be kind enough to look at both documents together with the enclosed budgets and let me know, in due course, what the possibilities might be regarding financial help.

I would welcome, needless to say, a chat with you in London next week. In the meantime, I do hope that you are enjoying your new position and that you will still have the odd occasion for a game of golf.

With kindest regards

Yours sincerely

Cyril McElhinney

PROPOSAL

SHANKILL YOUTH GROUP LURGAN
Parent and Child Training (PACT) Project
AIM: To serve young people in the context of the family.

CHILDREN IN TODAY'S WORLD

Children and their parents face an increasingly bewildering world. The pace of life becomes ever more rapid, and childhood, once a period of gradual learning and growth, is now bombarded with messages, ideas, and beliefs, which threaten the process of childhood, and turn children into consumer markets and advertising targets. Without sufficient support and guidance, children can all too easily become prey to unscrupulous sellers. However with the right support children can learn to weigh up situations and make clear and often perceptive judgements about their own needs and the needs of others. The Parish of Shankill in Lurgan believes that it has developed a scheme to support children and their parents in coming to terms with the world they inhabit. In helping to develop the full potential for children – physical, mental and spiritual – and by so doing encourage positive Christian morals and social values which will benefit and enrich community life in the years to come.

THE TOWN OF LURGAN

Background details on the town and its particular characteristics.

SHANKILL PARISH

Background details on the parish, its problems and the various initiatives currently in place.

WORK WITH YOUTH

Shankill Parish established Shankill Youth Group in 1973 which was an umbrella organisation for all its youth activities. Since that time co-ordinated programmes have been devised and run continuously making extensive provision for children and young people. The main centre of this work is in St Andrew Youth Complex at the top of the town. Shankill Youth Group activities have always been run on an entirely voluntary basis catering currently for over 200 members every week. The programme also includes a large summer scheme involving over 600 children and young people led by 50 volunteers. The programme makes a significant contribution to youth provision in the wider Lurgan area and in recognition of this receives grant aid from the Southern Education and Library Board on the costs of lighting, heating and equipment. Shankill Youth Group, through an effective and efficient Management Committee, has demonstrated its ability over the year to sustain a high quality youth provision for a wide range of young people in Lurgan and the surrounding areas.

It is through the experience and knowledge gained in this work that the Shankill Youth Group began to investigate how it could make an even more significant and positive impact on the lives of children and young people in Lurgan. We are very keen to develop a programme which would be relevant to all the community in Lurgan and so we are clear that any new development should have a cross community element. However we also believe that divisions should be addressed within the programme, and so we pinpointed the need to work with children not just on the basis of religion but also on economic background, and on gender. Our research indicated that many of the problems in the lives of young people especially those related to behaviour had already been established in earlier life. For that reason we decided to focus our project on the 5-10 age group, because we believe that earlier positive and more structured intervention in the lives of children will bring about significant benefits for them, their families and the community life.

THE PROPOSAL

Based on our research and investigation, Shankill Youth Group proposes to set up a pilot project which we believe is breaking new ground, and in relation to youth provision has a number of unique features:

(1) Development work with 5-10 year olds

The majority of provision for this age group operated loosely around a recreational structure. We believe that children in this age group, given the right support, are capable of problem solving and decision-making at a very sophisticated level. We want to harness and develop those skills in a positive way. We want to work with a broad range of children assisting them to develop personal action plans with the help of parents and family, to implement those plans, and to evaluate their successes and failures on a regular basis. These Personal Action Plans will contain achievable goals for a 12 month period concerning the social, physical and spiritual development of the children – thereby complementing the educational goals already established in the school. The process will be non competitive and will be an enjoyable experience for them and their families.

(2) Community relations in every sense

We intend through our networks to attract children to the Project from varying backgrounds. We believe that children can be very creative and open in their acceptance of differences, but often find their tolerance blunted and impaired by the environments in which they live. We want to support children in developing and enhancing their tolerance levels. Parents from both traditions will be encouraged to explore the causes of sectarianism in the community and to examine ways and means by which they can make a positive contribution which will help to ease tensions and to increase the level of understanding and tolerance in Lurgan. To achieve this in reality involves the third element of our Project.

(3) A whole family approach

The Project we propose can only succeed with the active involvement of parents whom we wish to integrate into the scheme as supporters working with their children – hence our chosen name Parent and Child Training – the PACT Project. As well as working with the children the Project will also work directly with parents, individually involving them in establishing realistic objectives for the development of the personal action plan for their own child's progress. It is recognised that successful outcomes are dependent upon their encouragement and active interest. Other members of the family will also be involved. The Project would also provide back-up support with workshops on parenting, homework, sickness and video games for example. In addition the Project will organise a number of family events throughout the year such as weekend camps, visits to pantomimes etc.

HOW WILL WE DO THIS?

Phase 1: Recruitment of staff and project advisers

Staffing will include a qualified youth worker, and information/research worker and administrative backup. In addition the Project wishes to recruit around 15 professionals from a number of fields including medicine, social work, education and special needs who

continued overleaf

will act as Project Advisers and who will agree to give their professional experience and advice when required.

In this phase the staff will begin to develop materials and resources for the Project and to develop networks and an information bank on facilities and services in the Lurgan area.

Phase 2: Recruitment of children/families

Using its already existing and substantial networks Shankill Youth Group will assist the staff in recruiting children to the scheme. We aim to have 100 children and their families involved in the first year.

Phase 3: Project implementation

Staff will begin to work with children to develop personal action plans and targets and to develop mechanisms for their regular review. Personal action plans will develop targets in all aspects of a child's life – home, school, community, social and recreational. Staff will also be developing a support programme for parents. We do not envisage the Project initiating activities for the children, but channelling them into the wide range of provision which already exists in the Lurgan area e.g. youth groups, sports clubs, leisure centres and church programmes. However, where we identify gaps in provision then we would seek to develop programmes to meet these needs. We are aware for example that cultural and artistic activities are not well catered for in the area, and are looking into this.

The Project will operate from the Church Walk premises which are adjacent to the town centre and regarded as 'neutral'. Once they come on the programme, we envisage children staying on PACT for at least three years to gain maximum benefit.

MANAGEMENT OF PACT

The Project will be managed by a 10 person committee appointed by Shankill Youth Group, and with power to co-opt three additional members. The committee will be representative of a wider community and will meet at least 6 times per annum. The Project will be managed on a day to day basis by the youth worker who will receive supervision and support from the Shankill Parish Co-ordinator.

EVALUATION

We see this Pilot Project running on a three year basis, and during this period we will regularly review our practice in the light of experience and learning. We are aware of the difficulties of evaluation. It is for this reason that we have decided to invite the University of Ulster team which would comprise academics with expertise in evaluation and in developmental psychology. Beyond that, we believe that a project as innovative as this one requires recording and a more structured approach to measuring the benefits. We will also be mindful that this is a model which can be replicated by other groups in different cities and towns in Northern Ireland. We feel it necessary to have the University directly involved in assisting us to ensure that we have a model which will work for others as well as for ourselves. It will also require to be cost effective.

For further information contact:
(*Details given*)

Budget
(*Detailed budget totalling around £175,000 for the three years*)

Follow-up letter

5 May 1993

Dear John,

It was good to meet you again at the Carnegie Inquiry into the Third Age Conference in London last week. I am sure you must be very pleased with the outcome. I know that I certainly was privileged to be there and to catch a real 'glimpse' of the issues. It will help us in Lurgan as we develop our response to many of the issues affecting the third age groups in our local community. I have noted that the Trust is not yet considering applications for funding to projects in this regard until later on in the autumn.

Further to our conversation in London, with regard to PACT, which we are hoping to implement on 1 August, there are some points which I want to clarify in response to your letter to me. It is intended to secure the support of a number of financial partners in the Project. To this end, the Southern Health and Social Services Board, the Southern Education and Library Board and the Cross Community Council have clearly indicated their financial interest from the statutory sector. I have also had discussions with Barnardos in Northern Ireland (*names given*) inviting their organisation to participate as the lead voluntary children's agency. We are also making applications to other Trusts/Foundations such as yourselves. Because of the nature of the budget of the PACT Project we will need significant contributions from all potential donors to ensure that it is adequately financed.

PACT is an important initiative with major possibilities for other large churches in Northern Ireland. Not only is Shankill Parish Church, through the recently formed Shankill Parish Caring Association (a registered charity) initiating a major piece of social action with regards to parenting, but it is also crossing the religious divide in a town which has been devastated by major terrorist activity. It is the church giving leadership in the wider community. This pilot project therefore, is being developed with the view to having it replicated in many other towns throughout the Province. It is for this reason, that we are seeking a wide range of statutory and voluntary partners to give guidance and to ensure that there is an effective evaluation process. Towards this end we are inviting the University of Ulster to assist in this difficult area. We are thoroughly convinced that the outcome could have profound benefits, not only for parenting and families, but also for community relations in Northern Ireland.

The support of the Carnegie United Kingdom Trust would add considerable status to the Project. I do hope, therefore, that you are able to assist us. I would also welcome, of course, a visit from yourself if you are in Northern Ireland to discuss any further details of PACT.

In the meantime I look forward very much to hearing from you.

With kindest regards

Yours sincerely

Cyril McElhinney

- The programme would be evaluated by an outside agency from the beginning to ensure that the objectives were being met and that, in a very sensitive location, both communities were being treated fairly.

Example 4

A quality idea with a credible management and good presentation

The Trust very rarely supports any kind of research. If it does, it has to be rooted in practical success and result in recommendations for wider good practice.

This application from Cities in Schools, therefore, had to be particularly convincing to trustees, especially as it was going to be considered at a meeting where there were very heavy demands on the trust's funds.

The first and last pages (*reproduced here*) made a powerful impact.

The first page:
- gave a clear purpose
- showed why CiS should do the work
- demonstrated that CiS was a credible, in fact, an outstanding organisation
- identified gaps in provision
- recommended an approach to the issue which coincided with the Trust's own approaches
- indicated CiS was familiar with evaluation process
- showed the project could have national impact
- above all demonstrated that the project was working in a field of real concern to the trustees.

The last page clearly identified the possible outcomes, which included dissemination.

The remainder of the application (not reproduced here) expanded on the methodology and resources needed.

Trust staff checked with an adviser to the Trust very familiar with the field who confirmed the impressions of the organisation and the potential significance of the proposal. Normally, the trustees would only give at most a small grant to research. In this case, they gave more than might have been expected.

Example 4

Proposed Cities in Schools Research 1996-1999: Tackling Social Exclusion

Purpose

To outline proposed research into the characteristics of the excluded population and the effectiveness of CiS work on reintegration in order to validate a model of good practice to be applied nationally.

Background

CiS is the only national charity working solely with children and young people who, through exclusion or long term non-attendance, are completely outside of mainstream education. There are approximately 150,000 14-17 year olds who fall into this category in the UK.

In the last three years the CiS network has grown from 3 to over 100 projects. The organisation's focus during this period has been on establishing operational credibility through implementing effective projects that re-integrate young people into schools and FE colleges.

Although CiS evaluates all its projects annually, resource constraints have meant that these evaluations concentrate on student performance during the project, academic achievement and initial destinations. More extensive research would enable agencies to:

(i) identify those most at risk of exclusion

(ii) assess those most easily re-integrated

(iii) evaluate the longer term impact of CiS projects.

Research gaps

While social exclusion for young people has moved rapidly up the policy and research priorities nationally, relatively little is known about these young people who challenge our schools and agencies and cost local communities a great deal.

More significantly, what research there is tends to map failure; there is no work that assesses all the needs of children and families who are not gaining access to mainstream services, particularly education. Equally, there is no body of research to underpin a model of good practice that could be used to have a national impact in terms of both policy nationally and practice locally.

In the context of the strategic development of CiS, this research would give unequivocal evidence of the effectiveness of the multi-disciplinary model and enhance significantly the quality of practice within existing projects.

Intended outcomes of CiS research

At the end of the programme, CiS will have:

(i) validated models of good practice that are applicable nationally for the reintegration of 5-19 year olds who are socially excluded;

(ii) established a profile of the multiple problems of socially excluded young people and their families;

(iii) designed and implemented a computerised management information system;

(iv) disseminated the findings nationally;

(v) influenced key policy makers in central government departments.

Martin Stephenson
Chief Executive

8 Writing a Better Application

Worked examples

This chapter analyses some genuine applications which have been sent to real funders. We aim to be constructively critical and suggest ways in which they could be improved. Each application letter is reproduced, although some have been slightly modified to disguise the true identity of the organisation. We also provide a commentary to highlight some key points.

There are a number of lessons to be gained from reading through these annotated examples:

- Once an application is written, it is often easy to improve on it. Read your first draft, get others to read it, and produce a much better second (and final) draft.
- Most applications that are sent are not particularly good. They are impersonal circulars, impassioned pleas without sufficient evidence to make a good case, a hotchpotch of half thought-through ideas; or they are sent to someone who is unlikely to be interested (the applications here are generally much better than most). Writing a good application gets you off to a good start.
- Read through a range of applications. That puts you in a similar position to a donor – you will have a lot to read about projects you know little about. Which would you fund if you had a limited grants budget at your disposal? Understanding the process from the donor's point of view can only be helpful.
- Finding the correct people to write to is as important as getting the message right.

All the examples shown here are good attempts by people working for successful projects that they believe in. We hope they take our comments in the positive context we intended!

Example 1 – A wasted opportunity

Here is a letter to a company asking for prizes to be donated for the charity's spring draw. It has certain merits. For example:

- it is a good length
- it recognises the company's desire for publicity

Example 1

A personalised letter sent to a number of companies from a major national charity

10th September

Dear Mrs Higgins,

Each year we run an Autumn Draw in order to raise money for the work of *** Charity. The draw is one of our most important sources of income, enabling us to provide vital support, advice and help for the five million or so people of all ages in the UK with ***, including more than 12,000 children. We do this through our 650 branches; groups for young disabled people; hotels and residential homes; and counselling and information services. We have several branches in Merseyside [where the company is based] and many of your customers and staff will have a first hand knowledge of the disease.

As 1995 is our 50th anniversary, we will be holding a special Golden Anniversary Draw. Suitable prizes will be crucial to its success and as we rely on donations. If you could help us by donating a prize we would be extremely grateful.

We will, of course, acknowledge your generosity through press releases, our own newspaper, *What's Going On?* (the best-read publication of its type, going to 100,000 people) including a special souvenir edition, and acknowledgement on the 2 million tickets we will have printed (in mid-October).

In our 50th anniversary year, the combined activities of celebration, fundraising and campaigning at all levels will provide *** Charity and its sponsors with a significant boost to public awareness and support. We are planning several major activities that will generate considerable media interest.

Any help and support you could offer would be greatly appreciated.

Yours sincerely,

Richard H. Smibbs
Events & Exhibitions Manager

- it tries to tie the charity in with the company by showing a geographical and personnel connection.

However, it could be so much better.

Firstly, this should be a very prestigious affair. A major celebratory year, potentially massive publicity across a wide cross-section of the population and lots of branches to ensure that the two million tickets are sold. Yet the letter is written just one month before the tickets are due to be printed. All this could have been sorted out well in advance. Furthermore, the whole thing should have been presented as a major sponsorship opportunity, rather than merely 'please donate a prize'.

Secondly, the funder has no real idea of the kind of prize required. How many are supposed to be awarded? What was given by whom last year? Did the charity have a particular company product in mind?

The letter says that the draw is a key part of the charity's fundraising. So how much does it raise? A lot of money, no doubt. Again, this could be a real selling point because at little cost to the company (missing out on one sale) the donation could help generate a massive amount of money. This could show terrific leverage.

There are some presentation problems. The first paragraph is very long and rather uninspiring. Why don't they get a user to say how wonderful the charity is or sign up a celebrity appeal patron to say the same thing – anything which makes the appeal a bit more exciting.

The third paragraph offers the company a range of benefits. Because they are all crammed into one sentence, they get a bit lost. Why not separate them out into bullet points?

The point of the fourth paragraph is not clear. Is the charity trying to offer the company further sponsorship opportunities? If so, what are they? Also, what is the centre-piece of the year of celebration (royal visit or whatever)? A carrot could be dangled about this.

Example 2 – Voluntary but not amateur

This application is a real shame because it doesn't do justice to the college or its users. It has many key faults.

It is a circular letter, so would almost certainly be binned straight away. Remember the old cliché: fundraising is friend-raising. If you can't be bothered to write a personalised letter, the recipient is hardly likely to think 'Terrific, I'd love to help these people'. You don't write circular letters to your friends; so why are funders different?

Furthermore, the writer doesn't want to speak to the funder. Rather, the reader is passed onto the college administrator. It implies that the writer is too busy or too exalted to speak to mere funders. This doesn't leave a good impression.

The tone of the letter is about how the college has struggled against all odds to run the course. This gets you down after a bit, doesn't it? Why not be really upbeat, showing how the college has achieved all this for minimal cost and that it is now ready to go onto the next stage of its development. They could show how many people have gone onto paid employment from the IT course. Or get a testimony from someone who has tried other forms of training and got nowhere; but then they came to the college and achieved wonderful results. Or show how the college releases the talents of the community that nobody else can. There must be lots of good stories to tell, so tell them (or at least one!); it will be more productive than talking about life's problems.

The application doesn't present any meaningful list of needs (other than to say they want everything). If the college doesn't want to say

---

Example 2

A circular letter which was photocopied and neither dated nor signed

Dear Sir/Madam,

The Southern College is an independent, charitable organisation, whose aim is to provide free education and training to the unemployed adults in the north end of the city. As a charity, we seek funding from many sources and much of the work of the college is undertaken by volunteers.

You can see from our leaflet that we do provide a very wide range of courses – a remarkable achievement given our limited resources.

However, at the Southern College the provision of I.T. training is limited. Size and scheduling of sessions is dictated by the hardware/software availability and the provision of tutor hours and there is a continual waiting list of student names.

At the moment we are in urgent need of computer hardware i.e. CPU's, monitors, keyboards, printers, peripherals, cables, mice, mats etc. We run 9 sessions per week (4 of these sessions are taught by volunteers) and we have a variety of machines, all of which are very, very old and well used.

In a society, where by the end of this century 80% of employment opportunities will require computer literacy, and, where Bill Gates predicts that in just two decades the majority of the working population will simply power up their computers to report for work, nobody can undermine the importance of training individuals in I.T. skills. Irrespective of how close these predictions are to the truth, there is no doubt that computers are playing an increasingly more central role in the education and employment markets.

In conclusion, we would appreciate any equipment, you could contribute, which will enable us to continue this valuable work. The college administrator is *** and she can be contacted on ***.

You [*sic*] faithfully

Richard H. Smibbs

'We need eight Apricot VS550s' (because they don't want to narrow the field unduly), they could at least say which programmes they want to train people in (WordPerfect 6 or whatever). They also need to be more specific about numbers (how many terminals, keyboards etc?).

A fundamental problem is the issue of revenue funding. If the college cannot afford mouse mats, why should they be able to run an educational programme?

Two final points. Firstly, why quote Bill Gates as an authority and then say he might be wrong? Secondly, the whole letter is about IT training. Yet on the enclosed brochure, IT is buried on side two, a single course among many and sandwiched between the Children's & Adult Drama Workshop and Tracing Your Family Tree. Hardly the best way to convince the funder that IT is as important as the letter tries to make out.

There is nothing wrong with needing more resources or showing that you have operated really effectively on a shoestring. Indeed, there is a thin line between being overly and underly 'professional' – unfortunately, this appeal definitely falls into the latter camp.

Example 3 – One thing or the other

This is an appeal from a medical research charity. It realises that it is hard to get wide scale company money for straight medical research and so, quite rightly, positions this as a public information campaign. However, once again the appeal makes some major mistakes.

Firstly, and fundamentally, it tries to combine two appeals as one. It asks for support both for the postcards to young people and for the GP/health professionals programme. These are two completely different markets. There are a whole range of companies who would be interested in the youth and student market. Are these companies really also going to be interested in GPs? Aren't these the preserve of drugs manufacturers and other health-orientated companies?

One approach may be to put together a really strong, upbeat proposal about new ways of warning of the dangers of the illness. The postcards could work really well, but should be placed in a positive context. The letter's tone suggests 'Oh, it's all very difficult you know'. Why not take the simple line that if people know what to look out for then half the battle is won? Tell a short story about someone who recognised the symptoms early and therefore received quick, successful treatment.

The company needs to be told what they stand to get out of all of this. Where does the proposed £350 fit into the £150,000 total? Why ask the company to pay 0.2% of the required sum? What good does this do? What recognition will the company get out of this?

Why not put together a formal sponsorship proposal based on the postcards? Presumably there will be thousands printed (although this is not stated) and there will be an effective distribution mechanism. The company's logo could be on each card so would gain it access to a key market. You could even try tying up with a band or night club to get the message better noticed. An alternative to concentrating on the postcards could be to produce a 'wish list' of different publicity options for the company to choose from, each clearly targeted at a particular market.

The GP/health professional leaflet should be an entirely separate proposal, again based on a sponsorship (of the information packs, for example).

Example 3

A letter to a locally-based company, personalised but with the reference 'cs/comp/gen', which rather belies the personal approach

Many families in your area have experienced the sudden trauma of *** over the past year. *** is one of the most dangerous of all medical conditions, affecting adults and children alike.

*** Charity is the only major UK charity which focuses solely on the funding of public awareness programmes and vital scientific research as a means to combat *** and which actively involves families affected by the disease in its work.

As you may be aware *** is notoriously difficult to diagnose. Yet with early identification it can often be successfully treated and leaves fewer victims scarred or disabled by their experience. The *** Charity therefore devotes a proportion of its resources to raising public awareness of the signs and symptoms of the disease. There is still a great deal of work that can be done and I hope [company name] will consider supporting the Charity's work. I enclose a copy of the Charity's annual review.

The cases of *** have unfortunately been on the increase with young people. In 1995, there was a two fold percentage rise in notifications of *** in teenagers and young adults. Currently information resources about these diseases for young adults are scarce and consequently this winter the Charity will launch a specific youth orientated initiative. Postcards, which are currently used to promote bands and night clubs, will be employed as an accessible medium to promote awareness of the signs and symptoms of *** to young adults. Once produced, the Postcards will be distributed to universities, colleges, clubs and restaurants to ensure young adults can access life saving information on ***.

Another important target group for the winter awareness programme is GP's and health professionals. We aim through the development and distribution of new literature to increase understanding of *** that often accompanies *** and is responsible for the majority of deaths.

To ensure the awareness programme is effective, we need financial backing. Greater public and professional awareness of *** will save lives. In the past companies have been very generous with an average donation of £350. The Foundation is budgeted to spend £150,000 on awareness programmes during the 1996/97 financial year. If you require any further information about the awareness campaigns or the research that we are funding, please do not hesitate to contact me.

I look forward to hearing from you in the near future.

Yours sincerely,

Alan Partridge
Fundraising Officer

Also, the company does not need to know about the gradual improvements in a very difficult medical area. It needs to understand the importance of the problem and that something practical and helpful can be done with its money. The application should describe the PR opportunity rather than simply attempt to sell a medical case.

Finally, there's a strong need for getting an editorial pen to this proposal. Although the above suggestions would change the content quite radically anyway, half the application could effectively be condensed into the following: 'Sadly, the incidence of *** is still on the rise. This is particularly the case with young people (where referrals doubled in 1995). However, the good news is that our researches show that when people can recognise the symptoms, the number of cases is halved (or whatever). We are launching an exciting new initiative to raise awareness about the disease among young people.' The focus could then move onto the postcards, how wonderfully effective they will be in raising awareness and the terrific publicity opportunity they present.

Example 4 – But what difference would we make?

This letter is from a celebrity. It is generally well-written, if a little long-winded. It certainly makes a compelling case, although no doubt some funders would question some of the statistics (is it really true that only 2% of people re-offend? How long after the end of the course were the figures compiled?) Generally the project comes over as being well-run and highly effective. The application contains some basic errors, however, all of which could have been easily avoided.

It's a mail-merged circular. The letter was undated; side two had been pre-printed (including a photocopied signature) onto a roll of computer paper (with the tell-tale perforations top and bottom). So, as a circular it would probably have been binned.

It's a shame that the celebrity didn't actually sign the letter. She is well-known and greatly respected for her community involvement and a personally signed letter from her would give the appeal tremendous weight.

The PS is problematic on two grounds. Firstly, these kinds of PS are best suited to direct mail, and its presence reinforces the impression of a mass mailing rather than a personal letter. Secondly, it suddenly introduces a negative tone, very much out of keeping with the rest of the letter. Why say that the whole future 'is at stake'? It creates doubt in the mind of the donor. If the work is as successful as the letter makes out, there is every reason to assume that the project will go from

Example 4

This letter is written by a celebrity about a project she is involved with

In the past you have generously supported the work of *** Foundation, for which we are deeply grateful. Your kindness has allowed over 1,000 people to complete the *** Foundation course, and the results have been remarkable.

I know what it is to plumb the depths of despair. But you don't have to go through what I went through for despair and apathy to take over. Apathy is a problem and it is a killer. It numbs the senses and crushes the spirit. It suffocates self-esteem, blights hope, freezes compassion. Apathy is the product of defeat, and people in our non-functioning inner cities know all about defeat. Many of them are third generation unemployed. Any dreams of success or fulfilment they cherished at school are shattered the moment they leave. Is it any wonder that the first steps to cynicism and alienation start at the school gates.

Almost one million young people are unemployed; 2,874,000 people under 19 live in a household dependent on supplementary benefit and 43% of known offenders are under 21.

You may think this sounds like a lost cause, that the possibility of hauling any young person out of so dire an environment is so slight as to be hopeless. Here at *** Foundation we don't believe in hopelessness, we firmly believe that just because someone has never been given hope it doesn't mean they haven't got any.

A recent survey shows that of the young people who undertook *** Foundation course 42% have found full time employment, 47% have returned to education and 100% undertook a community benefit project. Home Office statistics show that young people who first convict at an early age are more likely to continue offending. 65% of young people had admitted to breaking the law before joining *** and after their involvement with us only 2% have re-offended.

We have shown through the remarkable successes we have had with young people who have undertaken our course, that there is hope and a future for today's youth. Yet there is so much for us still to do – existing centres in *** require expansion to deal with ever-increasing numbers that are being referred to us. New centres need to be established – particularly in ***. Services need to be expanded, but all this requires additional funding.

That is why I am writing to you today, to ask if you will support our national appeal, and raise the £500,000 we need, to give hope and aspiration to more of today's youth.

It costs just £1,500 to fund one young person to go on our course – compare that to the £16,000 a year it costs to keep a young person locked up. A gift of £100 today could radically change the course of a person's life.

The sooner we reach our target, the sooner we can provide the vital work that *** Foundation is renowned for, to communities with high unemployment, high crime and low academic achievement. Please give as much as you can so we can provide a future filled with hope and self-worth for more and more people.

I would like to take this opportunity of wishing you a Happy Christmas, from all the members and staff at *** Foundation, and thank you for your support.

Yours sincerely,

Grace Ellington

PS The enclosed letter from Mary, one of our members sums up in her own words the life of despair she was living before she went on the *** course. The future of young people like Mary and that of *** Foundation is at stake. Please help us to secure both.

strength to strength. Try to inspire people to give money, not emotionally bribe or frighten them.

There is also a problem with the way the letter asks for money. Firstly, there is confusion. Are they asking for part of the £500,000 (which is presumably mainly capital expenditure, although this is not clear) or do they want the donor to pay for individual young people at £1,500 a year? They should ask for one or the other, but not both.

If you are going for the £500,000-style approach then you need to have raised some of that total privately before going public (the general rule is get about 25% committed by key donors before opening the appeal up more widely). Give the impression that the appeal has bags of momentum already. Also, you would need to show where the money is coming from and how much you expect trusts, companies or whoever to put in. By breaking everything down into smaller units (say giving yourself a target of £20,000 from companies, £40,000 from trusts, £75,000 from fundraising events etc.), you give the impression that (i) the contribution you are asking for in the letter is much more significant, and (ii) the whole thing is much easier.

Alternatively, if you want £1,500 per person a year, why ask for £100? It doesn't even cover one month's costs. Where does this amount come from? If you are approaching companies, why not set up a friends' scheme whereby they notionally adopt one young person. Or have a corporate members' club whereby you try to recruit W gold members, X silver members, Y bronze members and Z ordinary members. Obviously, the amount each pays comes down as you come down the hierarchy and the benefits you offer increase as you go up. If you are doing this, again you will need to get some members signed up in private first. You need to give the impression in your letter that the company stands to miss out if they don't act now.

Finally, the recipient of this letter had never actually funded the project before. The first line therefore makes a pretty bad impression.

Example 5 – But where's the evidence?

This letter is a circular about a community regeneration project. The project itself has done some really good work, although the potential funder (or 'partner' in this case) would need to do their own research to find this out.

The basic idea behind the proposal is a sound one. If the project can get enough members together this will achieve two things:

- it will make the project self-sustaining without recourse to further fundraising;
- it will build a strong constituency of support for its future work which greatly increases its influence.

Example 5

Dear Friend and Partner

As you know *** is committed to the concept of regeneration and renewal within our inner city – but to so much more as well. Set up some eighteen months ago, it has developed its remit to 'promote and encourage the further development of the Back Lane Area', an area defined by the City Council as including not only Back Lane, but also Side Street, Main Street and the Museum. *** has the potential to engineer further cultural and urban renewal: – to build upon the imagery which Back Lane engenders, to promote the locality as a powerhouse for the performing arts and to enhance its ambience for all those who live, work, and study in our city.

It has already established itself as an innovator, facilitator and coordinator, preparing blueprints for development and encouraging cooperation between disparate agencies. It has a vision which is realistically achievable and which will be to the great advantage of our city and its people.

Consultant advisers have given freely of their time and expertise, local residents and businesses have been enthusiastically involved and the support of the cathedral and the universities has been unswerving.

Until now expenses have been covered by contributions from City Challenge and a wide range of organisations, businesses and individuals committed to the locality. Whereas *** remains firmly within the voluntary sector, it is inevitable that it will face significant expenditure if it is to purposefully and realistically pursue its goals.

It was in recognition of this that last month's Annual General Meeting determined that there should be an annual subscription for partners, be they businesses or individuals. I do hope that you will be able to offer financial support. The *** project is both spectacular and momentous. It offers great opportunity for our city as it approaches the new millennium. It must not fail.

Yours faithfully,

Richard H. Smibbs

However, the letter is unlikely to succeed, partly because it is a circular, but also because it makes various claims and several key assumptions without backing any of them up with evidence. For example, 'The project is both spectacular and momentous'. Does the application say why? 'It offers great opportunity for our city as it approaches the new millennium.' For instance...? 'It has a vision which is realistically achievable and which will be to the great advantage of our city and its people.' Excellent, but what is it?

The project assumes that the recipient is already keen and knows a lot about what has been going on. This is a very dangerous assumption. Even when you know someone really well, the general fundraising rules still apply – make your case by showing what needs to be done and how you will do it.

This letter is positive and enthusiastic. However, it needs more specifics, some really good examples of what has been and what will be done, and a sense that a lot of local people and organisations had already joined together to do something (you could get the keenies to sign up first, highlight their support in the letter, and then list all of them in any supporting material). The letter also needs personalising, of course!

Example 6 – Discovering a hidden pearl

Many organisations have an aspect of their work which is so interesting, so effective or perhaps such a brilliant solution to a known problem, that getting support will not be a problem.

But often, the proposal masks the basic idea which will attract donors. Or perhaps the proposal writer simply has not recognised the value of the work being done. The day-to-day running of the project takes up all the energy, and does not allow the project organiser to step back and see the project in its proper perspective.

This application from the Northtown and District Advice Project seems just another proposal for running costs to support a worthy community project. Another good cause which, in a crowded fundraising market, is likely to have difficulty in attracting the support it needs. But hidden amongst all the detail (which is anyway far too great for most donors) is a really interesting proposition. Consider the following points.

1. Northtown is an area of high unemployment, poverty and all the consequential problems that stem from this. This point could easily be documented by statistics.
2. Each year Northtown's advice service has enabled local residents to claim additional benefits of around £500,000. Remember these were benefits they were entitled to but had not claimed or obtained. This is also a cumulative process. Every year more and more people are helped and more benefits are taken up. This figure is approximate; it was obtained by follow-up of clients advised by the Centre in order to evaluate the impact of the advice.
3. Because the service is run by unemployed people themselves, it is an extremely low-cost service. It will also be by definition user-friendly. It costs just £12,900 to run the project each year and a major local trust is picking up more than half the tab.
4. The multiplier effect is enormous. Helping this project must be one of the most effective and cost-effective (for the donor) ways of relieving poverty in a poor neighbourhood. Advising clients on their welfare entitlements and enabling them to take up the benefits that

---

Example 6

Form letter on the word processor, personalised before being sent out from the Northtown & District Advice Project

Re: Application for Operating Costs & Volunteers Expenses 95/96

Northtown & District Advice Project has been operating since April 1994. This Project is the result of local people responding to the desperate need for an advice service in their neighbourhood. Since opening, the Project has been very successful and has achieved its aims of providing advice on Welfare Rights and Housing. Although other advice facilities exist, distance and travel costs are an important factor for many sections of the population. To be effective, advice services must be located where need is greatest and if necessary offer an out-reach service to the people in their homes.

While Welfare Rights and Housing account for the majority of enquiries, a number of people need help over a far wider range of troubles, i.e. Income Tax, Hire Purchase Debts, Racial Harassment, Victims of Violence, Domestic Problems. Clients have also been represented at a number of tribunals. This can take up far more time than can realistically be given by volunteers. Some of the people who call in, do not come under any particular category, but call in for somebody to talk to, to relieve the pressures they are living under in their present environment.

At present the Advice Project is open for five, two hour sessions per week and deals with, on average, twenty enquiries per session. Approximately two thirds of these are, or become on going cases. As a result of the Project many people have benefited by an increase in their weekly amounts, by receiving back dated money or by single payments. Other categories of work in the main involve Housing and Fuel disconnections. A significant number of those using the Project are from ethnic minorities. When the Project first started the percentage of such people using it was very small, it is now in the region of 50%.

The Project is staffed by volunteers from the Northtown area. Each advice worker has undergone training in Welfare Rights and receives expenses for the work they undertake. As the volunteers live in the area advice is requested from them in the streets, shops and pubs, etc. as much as when they are in the 'shop'.

The development of the Advice project has been supported by Northtown Community Project, a community work project set up by The Children's Society. The Advice Project operates from the Northtown Community Project shop premises. In addition to the use of the premises (including heating and lighting) Northtown Community Project also provides administrative support and assistance from the community work staff. Running costs have been met through donation from Charitable Trusts totalling £12,200 for 1994/95.

The Advice Project needs £12,900 to operate for the financial year 1995/96. The John Moores Foundation have agreed to grant £7,200 having this leaves a shortfall of £5,700 which we are trying to cover through applications to charitable trusts. Any support you can give will be greatly appreciated.

Yours sincerely,

Adrienne Wainwright

(*Statistics and project details enclosed*)

are due to them is 40 times more effective than giving cash handouts to those in greatest need.

5. A welfare system with targeted benefits requires good advice to those in need if it is to work. An advice service such as this one maximises the contribution of the State as well as maximising the impact of the much smaller charitable resources of the donor.

6. Every community should have a service like this! A proper evaluation of the project and a development programme to export the idea into other areas could be the subject of a further application for funding.

Convinced? You should be. Here is a really good project which deserves support. Unfortunately, the fundraising application does not bring all this out.

Examine your own organisation and the work it is doing. Is there a hidden pearl there? Is there an idea so good that donors will rush to fund you once you have explained to them what you are doing and how much you need to do it with? If there is, you should have no problems!

Examples 7 and 8 – Building on a local connection

Not every donor will be interested in your work. This is particularly true for local projects seeking support from a company where there almost always needs to be a local connection.

Example 7 was an obviously circular letter, with the addressee written in by hand at the top of the page. It is short and clearly laid out – so far, so good. But the writer makes a number of assumptions – that Kodak (based in Hemel Hempstead) has an interest in improving the living conditions of a Sheffield community; that Kodak could somehow 'improve its profile' by investing in community development; and lastly, that Kodak can make a significant contribution to a very large budget.

This is a typical letter where an applicant has not understood – or even bothered to find out about – the grants policies of the donor, and has simply assumed that because the charity is short of money a large company would be interested in giving it.

The second letter, from Hammersmith and Fulham Amenity Trust (example 8), recognises the importance of the local connection and uses an opportunity from the company chairman's publicly-stated concern to start the grants process moving. Because the company is a very large local employer with long historic ties in the borough, the trust is obviously seeking a large grant. To this end, the first step is to build a

---

Example 7

To R Miller of Kodak Ltd from the Chairman of Eastside Community Association/Action Group

Dear Sir,

I am writing to you on behalf of the above mentioned voluntary organisation.

Eastside is a rapidly developing Community situated on the boundary of Sheffield and whose village services are at present under immense strain. To overcome the problem the Action Group was formed with a view to developing a new Community Centre based on the conversion of the now vacant local Vicarage.

A project report showing an Architects proposed design and costings for the scheme is enclosed for your perusal.

The self help group now need the backing for this Centre which is badly needed to provide facilities especially for the under 5s and senior citizens. We need a total of £196,000, and are looking for financial support from your good selves for which we in return can enlarge your company profile and market awareness in a rapidly developing new township.

Obviously any help in this project would be gratefully received and any conditions imposed on sponsorship we would endeavour to meet.

However we must emphasise the urgency of our request and look forward to receiving your early reply.

Thanking you in anticipation.

Yours faithfully,

Richard Fuller

---

relationship, rather than ask for a donation. The letter is the first step; then a phone call; then, hopefully, a meeting to discuss how the trust and the company might work in partnership; and only then, an application for support.

Example 9 – Humility will not always pay

With a continuous need to look for money, many charities humble (or humiliate) themselves, present themselves as worthy but victims of circumstance, and adopt a begging bowl approach to fundraising.

This approach may work sometimes and with some donors, but it is an inherently unsatisfactory way of setting about fundraising. Most organisations are dealing with serious problems or meeting real need in an effective and professional way. The fact that they need financial help to do this is neither a criticism of the project nor should it create an inferiority complex. This can be counterproductive in fundraising, and it can also affect the attitudes and self-image of those who work for the charity.

Example 8

To Richard Fuller, Public Relations Manager of Fuller Smith and Turner from the Director of the Hammersmith and Fulham Amenity Trust

Dear Mr Fuller

UK2000 Thames Project – Environmental Improvements

I noted with pleasure that your chairman, Mr Anthony Fuller, represented Fullers at the UK2000 reception aboard the Elizabethan recently on July 28th, as it demonstrated your company's obvious concern for the environment. I am aware of your company's long association with our part of London, particularly the river, and in view of this I hope that we will be able to link up with you in some of our environmental projects.

Hammersmith and Fulham Amenity Trust was established in 1982 to make our borough a brighter and greener place to visit, work or live in and to create training and employment opportunities. The Trust is an independent charity which receives support from a variety of public and private bodies and carries out a wide range of work including landscape gardening, tree planting, and playgrounds combined with our training schemes for local unemployed people, and events such as the Thames Project. Our newsletter, annual report and other publications are designed to inform the public on green issues and promote a better environment.

Our work is initiated by individuals and groups representing residents, schools, housing associations, playgroups, local businesses, health authorities and the Council – all our projects involve local people in their design, implementation and maintenance after completion.

Currently we have a number of projects which your company may wish to support ranging from improvements to the riverside and canalside, to greening some of the borough's bleaker housing estates, a garden for a home for the elderly, a children's play area, tree and bulb planting in several locations.

I hope that your company would like to take the opportunity that the Trust presents to become more closely associated with improving the quality of our environment and I will contact you shortly to discuss further details.

Yours sincerely,

R. Miller

(*annual report and newsletter enclosed*)

Take example 9 which is a very well-regarded national charity moving its head office. This move should be seen as an opportunity to build a successful future, not a victim of the legal circumstances of its property tenure.

The cost of the move is trivial (£30,000). Some of the funders being approached would not even notice this figure in the amounts they budget when they move head office. It is also a tiny amount in relation to the value of the work being done by the organisation and in relation to the opportunities for its future development.

The humble approach has also led the organisation to ask for too little ('moderate contributions of a few hundred pounds from each of a number of Companies and Trusts'). This will make the job of fundraising that much harder. Over 50 donors will have to say yes for the appeal to succeed. Surely it would be much better to make a much stronger case and seek larger donations from a more limited number of donors. This would also allow more time to be spent on persuasion and less reliance on a 'scatter gun' approach of sending essentially the same letter to several hundred potential donors in the hope that some might respond. It also means that good relations can be developed with a few while leaving other untapped sources for future fundraising.

People will want to support the appeal because this charity is doing a really good job, because toy libraries are a sensible and effective way of helping and enriching the lives of disabled children. The move is an excuse to ask for money for the valuable work of the organisation, but it is not the real reason why people will want to give it.

Example 9

A personalised letter sent to the grants secretaries and donations managers of a number of trusts and companies by the Chair of the Trustees

As a result of the enforced termination of our existing lease at Seabrook House, our Trustees have been obliged to seek alternative accommodation by the middle of June.

Fortunately, we have secured offices in Stephenson Way, Euston, London NW1, but the cost of actually moving will impose a considerable extra burden on our existing budget.

Every effort is being made to economise on other areas of expenditure, but such savings are unlikely to yield anything like the £30,000 required to cover the overall cost of the move, which involves everything from legal costs to the fixtures and fittings in the new premises.

With the exception of a DHSS grant, all funding has to be raised by voluntary means, and I enclose a series of leaflets outlining our charitable work on behalf of toy libraries throughout the British Isles, together with a copy of our most recently published accounts for 1994/95.

The financial position has not significantly changed within the last twelve months, and I am, therefore, urgently seeking moderate contributions of a few hundred pounds each from a number of Companies and Trusts who might be willing to help underwrite the costs of our move.

Our Appeals Officer, Elizabeth Archer, will be more than happy to provide added background information if required, but I profoundly hope my personal appeal for your support will be sympathetically considered by you or your Committee as appropriate.

Cheques should, of course, be made payable to *** Charity and I hope very much you will be able to respond favourably in due course.

Yours sincerely,

Jenny Merton

Example 10 – Keep it short and simple

There is often a tendency to put every little detail into an application. This should be resisted, as it makes the appeal much less effective

This appeal has a very simple story: a charity providing services for disabled people is running a number of successful activities, largely paid for out of statutory grants. It needs to put its accounts on computer. It has negotiated a good deal for doing this and it will save money in the long run. There is no need for the appeal letter to be so long – it could be halved!

Although the appeal is to improve the administrative efficiency of the organisation, it is the nature of the charity's work which will move the donor to give. Although this is described in an attached information sheet, it would be helpful to highlight the main work of the organisation, giving an indication of its size (number of beneficiaries, not staff) and highlighting some of its successes and achievements.

Example 11 – Stressing the benefits

With a sponsorship application, the company is interested in the benefits it will receive if it gives its support.

This letter sets out the benefits quite clearly – including the hidden benefit of doing something in ASDA's patch. Tesco, as a company, is promoting its healthy, caring and environmentally sound image. This project could fit well into this strategy.

However, the benefits as stated in this application have not really been quantified. How many people will visit the show? How much local publicity and press coverage will be generated? What other ways of meeting Tesco's needs are possible (for example, giving out discount vouchers to encourage people to visit the store)? An organisation seeking sponsorship should think carefully about the benefits, be as specific as possible and then see whether it is possible to make the proposition even more attractive to a potential sponsor.

Example 10

To the Manager of the local Marks & Spencer store from the Administrator of Southtown Disability Forum

Dear Miss Eastwood,

We are writing to enquire whether Marks & Spencer would consider making a donation towards the cost of purchasing an accounts programme for our computer.

Southtown Disability Forum (SDF) is an independent voluntary organisation established in 1973 to improve the quality of life of disabled people living and working in the Southtown. We are a registered Charity (Registration No: 123456) and a Company Limited by Guarantee (Registration No: 987654), and are run by an elected Management Committee of disabled people and their carers nominated by our membership.

We receive an annual grant from Southtown Council which covers some of the cost of employing 4 full-time and 1 part-time staff, rent and basic running expenses. We also receive a joint grant from the Health Authority and Social Services towards the funding of 1 full-time and 1 part-time post. All other costs are raised by ourselves.

SDF was recently successful in fundraising for a computer to help produce and update our wide range of publications, information sheets and newsletter as well as our mailing lists. This has proved beneficial to SDF not only in the improvement of delivery of services but also in the savings made in terms of staff time (freeing staff to do other work).

It has also highlighted the need to make our accounts more simplified and less time-consuming. Unfortunately in order to have the accounts on the computer we would need to purchase a separate accounts package. We are writing to ask if Marks & Spencer would consider funding SDF to enable us to purchase such a programme for our computer.

A former user of SDF's Advice and Information Service who is a Lecturer in Computer Programming has advised us that if we were to buy an accounts package called ABC95 he would be able to rewrite the programme and tailor it to SDF's individual needs. He has offered these services free of charge and if SDF buys the software package (total cost including VAT = £644) he is willing to make a donation of £150.00 towards the cost. This means that for £499.00 we can have an accounts programme which will not only enable us to be more efficient with staff time but will also eventually result in savings in account costs being made. We currently have to send our accounts to a Chartered Accountant who enters them onto a computer which costs approximately £300.00 a year.

Like any other Company we have to present detailed accounts for Audit purposes. However, in addition to these requirements we have to send quarterly and annual accounts to our funding bodies. More than ever we have to be able to produce up to the minute accounts or budgets either for the Company as a whole or for individual projects that we carry out. Our present manual system is both cumbersome and time-consuming. With the right kind of accounts package not only will it allow us to be more effective in presenting our accounts but will also free up the staff member currently responsible for SDF's Accounts to enable more fundraising work to be done.

I have included a precis of some of the work done by SDF as well as a copy of our last printed Annual Report which includes the Audited Accounts for 1995/96. It should be noted that the surplus carried forward from the previous year was due to staff vacancies and that SDF was allowed to retain these savings in order to help cover revenue costs in 1996/97 which were not met by grant aid. Since April 1995 our accounts have become more complicated due to receiving funding from more than one source.

If there is any further information that you require in order to consider the above please do not hesitate to contact me.

Yours sincerely,

Arnold Lane

(*One page information sheet on SDF and its work attached.*)

Example 11

To the Manager of the local Tesco Stores from a member of the Voluntary Management Committee of Northtown City Farm

Dear Mr Garbutt,

I am writing to offer you the opportunity of sponsoring an event at Northtown City Farm, a local project with which many of your staff and customers are no doubt familiar. I had originally approached ASDA as their Northtown store is just down the road from the Farm, but they have chosen to turn down a chance of gaining good publicity for themselves.

Northtown City Farm is an ambitious voluntary community project providing considerable social, recreational and educational benefits to local people in a whole range of activities extending way beyond the central farmyard. We cater for people of all ages, as you will see from the enclosed leaflet and Annual Report.

Many of our members (over 800 families) and local poultry breeders are pressing us to put on a Poultry Show, which we would like to do one Saturday in September if we can obtain financial support for it. I believe your Company would derive much benefit from sponsoring this event for several reasons.

1) Tesco would be able to promote its products and the local store by advertising at the show.

2) Tesco would enhance its caring image through its partnership with a popular community project enjoyed by hundreds of adults and children living in the area around the Brislington store.

3) Tesco would earn respect for joining with us in our efforts to bring a greater understanding of farming to city people. Many of our potential exhibitors are keen to show their poultry in the city for the same reason.

Our estimated costs for putting on the show (including hire of equipment, transport, publicity, judges expenses, prize money, staffing, insurance and other overheads) are £1,420. We are confident of the Show's success because of the interest already being shown and the enthusiasm of small local breeders who feel unable to show their birds at large agricultural shows but would welcome an opportunity to participate in a smaller event.

I should be delighted if Tesco Stores agreed to sponsor this year's event. You are very welcome to come and visit the Farm, and I would be pleased to answer any questions you may have. I look forward to hearing from you.

Yours sincerely,

Paula Ironside

9 Assessing Your Application

Few applications are perfect, even the ones that raise lots of money. Most can be significantly improved, and it is surprising how many miss out something of real importance.

Before you send off your application, it's worth checking it thoroughly, not just for spelling mistakes, but to make sure that all the details are correct and that you haven't missed out your key selling point or a vital piece of information.

This chapter aims to help you assess:

- How good is your application?
- How, if at all, might you improve it?

Have you written a good application?

Style

☑ **The title:** is the project title succinct, catchy, appropriate?

☑ **First paragraph:** does the first paragraph grab the reader's attention, create sufficient interest for the reader to continue with the proposal?

☑ **Writing:** are you happy with the way you have written this proposal? Does it read well?

☑ **Length:** is it the right length? Does it include all the key points you wish to make?

☑ **Tone:** is the proposal positive, confident, enthusiastic? Does it create a sense of urgency and importance for the project?

☑ **Logical flow:** is there a logical structure to the proposal going from problem to solution, from solution to the resources required to provide that solution, and from the resources you require to how the donor can help?

☑ **Visual impression:** is the proposal nicely laid-out with shortish paragraphs, sub-heads and tabulations (where appropriate)? Is it typed neatly and without spelling mistakes?

☑ **Letterhead:** are you happy with your organisation's letterhead? Is it visually attractive? Does it contain all the information it should?

Communication with the donor

☑ **Personal approach:** does the application give the impression of being a personal letter individually written to the donor? Is it signed personally?

☑ **Previous contact:** does the application mention previous approaches or any other contacts you may have had with the donor?

☑ **Donor interests:** is the proposal likely to be of interest to the donor, knowing what you do about their concerns and priorities?

☑ **Donor guidelines:** if the donor publishes guidelines for applicants, have you read these carefully, and does your application fall clearly within the guidelines?

☑ **Scale of request:** is your request reasonable, given what you know about the donor's scale of grant-making?

☑ **Rationale:** have you given good reasons why the donor should want to support the project? If writing to a company, have you clearly stated the benefits they will get from supporting you?

☑ **Empathy:** are you on the same wavelength as the donor? Or, if you are not, does the application build a bridge between your point of view and theirs?

☑ **Signatory:** is the signatory to the letter the most appropriate for the particular donor? And is he or she the first point of contact?

☑ **Follow up:** do you suggest any follow up if the proposal is of particular interest (a site visit, the supply of further and more detailed information, a meeting)?

☑ **Report back:** if you are seeking substantial support, do you indicate how and at what intervals you intend to report on progress?

...or a bad application?

Style

- ☒ **First paragraph:** is the first paragraph a turn off? Will the reader lose interest and read no further?

- ☒ **Writing:** is it dreary, verbose and stuffed with jargon, unsubstantiated superlatives, long sentences and unnecessarily long words?

- ☒ **Length:** is it over-long? Can you shorten it by cutting out unnecessary words? Have you tried to say too much?

- ☒ **Tone:** is the tone of the proposal hectoring or over-assertive? Is it whinging or apologetic? Or is it complacent?

- ☒ **Logical flow:** is the application a complete muddle? Do you dart from one point to another and back again? Do you repeat yourself?

- ☒ **Visual impression:** is the typing a mess? Are there spelling mistakes? Does it contain great chunks of unbroken text?

- ☒ **Letterhead:** have you got a massive letterhead which takes up half a page? Does it include out-of-date information (e.g. names of trustees who have moved on, are no longer MPs or whatever)? Is there any other problem with it?

Communication with the donor

- ☒ **Personal approach:** is the application a circular appeal? Does it give the impression of having been sent off to a large number of people (whether or not this is actually the case)?

- ☒ **Previous contact:** have you failed to mention any previous contact (even if you were turned down)?

- ☒ **Donor interests:** does the proposal fall completely outside the donor's known concerns and priorities? If so, why are you writing to them (you must have a really good reason)?

- ☒ **Donor guidelines:** have you forgotten to get hold of the guidelines? Have you not really read them, or deliberately misinterpreted them so that you fit in?

- ☒ **Scale of request:** does the scale of your need and your request fail to match the scale of the donor's grant-making? Are you looking for such a large sum that the donor can't really make a worthwhile contribution? Conversely, are you looking for such a small sum that the donor can't really be bothered?

- ☒ **Rationale:** do you just hope the donor may be interested, that by a process of osmosis they will understand the benefits of their support?

- ☒ **Empathy:** are you too radical or not radical enough, too establishment or not establishment enough, on the wrong network or wavelength?

- ☒ **Signatory:** has the application letter been signed by the fundraising assistant, or signed pp by the signatory's secretary? Does this give the impression that you can't really be bothered?

- ☒ **Report back:** will they next hear from you when you next want money?

Have you written a good application?

Content

☑ **Need:** have you made a good case (centred on your users) and supported it with a few relevant facts and figures?

☑ **Credibility:** have you established that your organisation has the ability, the particular skills and the other resources necessary to make an impact?

☑ **The proposal:** have you explained in clear, simple terms exactly what you propose to do? Is everything the donor needs to know included in the letter?

☑ **Project idea:** is the project likely to be seen as interesting, relevant, attractive to a donor?

☑ **Objectives:** have you set yourself specific and measurable objectives for the project? And are these reasonable given the level of staff time and resources at your disposal? Are you confident?

☑ **Evaluation:** do you intend to evaluate the outcome of your work and have you shown how you intend to set about doing this? Is this likely to be effective and is it being done at reasonable cost?

☑ **Dissemination:** if the proposal is for a pilot project, for research or action research, or to produce a publication, have you shown how you plan to disseminate the results, or what you have produced with the grant?

☑ **The offer:** have you made a specific request for support or given a clear indication to the donor as to how much you want them to give? Have you mentioned where the rest of the money is coming from, or who has already given to the appeal?

☑ **Future funding:** have you at least shown that you have thought about the future funding implications of the proposal (the running costs, or whatever) even though there may be no certain answers at this stage?

Budget

☑ **Arithmetic:** do the figures add up?

☑ **Costings:** have you included all the items of expenditure that you plan to incur? Are all the items costed realistically?

☑ **Overheads:** where appropriate, have you included an apportionment of overhead of administrative costs in your budget? Does the basis on which you have calculated this appear reasonable?

☑ **Value:** does the total cost appear to you to be reasonable in relation to the work you plan to do? Does the proposal represent value for the donor's money? Is this clear from what you have said?

☑ **Inflation:** if the project is to run over several years, have you made any allowance for inflation (or stated that the budget for future years does not take account of any inflation in costs)?

Supporting information

☑ **Finance:** have you included your annual accounts and a budget for the project?

☑ **Brochure:** have you got a suitable brochure or report to attach? Does it enhance what you say in the application? Is it nicely designed and illustrated?

☑ **Other:** is there any other information you could or should include?

...or a bad application?

Content

☒ **Need:** have you simply assumed that everyone knows what you are doing is important? Have you spoken in generalisations and made bland assertions?

☒ **Credibility:** have you assumed that everybody has heard about you, thinks well of you, and is convinced of your capabilities?

☒ **Proposal:** is your description of the project muddled? Incomplete? Are you expecting the donor to wade through loads of supporting material to get a proper idea of what you are trying to do.

☒ **Project idea:** have you made the project seem boring, old-fashioned, of marginal benefit?

☒ **Objectives:** have you failed to set objectives? Are they very generalised, couched in 'We hope this...' or 'We may do...'? Or are the objectives so grandiose that they become completely unrealistic?

☒ **Dissemination:** are you keeping everything to yourselves?

☒ **The offer:** have you mentioned some global fundraising target and simply asked for 'a generous contribution'? Have you given no indication of the scale of support you are looking for?

☒ **Future funding:** are you asking for running costs and giving no indication of how the project will continue in future years? Are you asking for an item of equipment or raising money for a building, without giving any indication of how the running costs will be met?

Budget

☒ **Arithmetic:** are there silly mistakes in your addition?

☒ **Costings:** have you forgotten to include certain items of expenditure? Are the figures just 'plucked out of the air'? Have you obtained any quotes or estimates for larger items of capital expenditure?

☒ **Value:** does the proposal seem a lot of money for what you plan to do?

Supporting information

☒ **Brochure:** is your supporting material written for internal consumption (as, say, a discussion document)? Is it written in long paragraphs, no sub heads, heavily jargonised? Is it overly glossy or does it look too cheap?

Assessing your application

Now assess your application on the following lines...

Factor	Satisfied? YES/NO	Action points
Style		
Title		
First paragraph		
Writing		
Length		
Tone		
Logical flow		
Visual impression		
Letterhead		
Communication with donor		
Personal approach		
Previous contact		
Donor interests		
Donor guidelines		
Scale of request		
Rationale		
Empathy		
Signatory		
Follow up		
Report back		

Factor	Satisfied? YES/NO	Action points
Content		
Need		
Credibility		
Proposal		
Project idea		
Objectives		
Evaluation		
Dissemination		
The offer		
Future funding		
Budget		
Arithmetic		
Costings		
Overheads		
Value for money		
Inflation		
Supporting information		
Finance		
Brochure		
Other		

10 Checklists and Fact Files

Serious fundraising requires serious record-keeping. Much of this involves getting information that is dispersed throughout the organisation (or lives only in people's heads) and putting it into a central file. This can be time-consuming. However, once you have done it (and as long as you keep updating it as you go) it is a fairly straightforward maintenance job.

The information you keep is entirely up to you. The following covers the various points and issues discussed in this book. Use it or adapt it as necessary.

Contents

1. Organisation fact file

The basic facts about your organisation, its aims and its history. Often this is forgotten.

2. Credibility fact file

Some basic information about the successes and achievements of the organisation, its main financial sponsors (whose support provides an endorsement) and note of any recent press and media coverage.

3. Credibility box file

A box file in which you keep endorsements; quotations; lists of patrons and financial sponsors; clippings from newspaper articles or research reports highlighting the problem or need; statistics and trends which demonstrate the full extent of the problem and how the situation is changing; evaluation reports which reflect the good work being done by the organisation; case studies and photographs that put a human face on your work; in fact anything that might be useful in reinforcing your case. Every organisation should have one!

4. Fundraising plan for the organisation

To help you plan your fundraising needs well in advance.

5. Project fact file

The basic facts about your project, its importance and how it will be run.

6. Budget checklist

To help you plan your expenditure requirements.

7. Fundraising plan for the project

To help you plan where and how you will raise the money you need for your project, and to develop contingency plans if you are not immediately successful.

8. Keeping track of progress

Checklists to record the grants and donations you receive and to track the progress of your more important applications.

9. Mobilising contacts

To help you identify the personal contacts and mobilise the support of your staff, trustees, patrons and others who can help you in your fundraising.

1. Organisation fact file

Last updated:

Name of organisation:

Address:

Date founded:

Why, how and by whom founded:

Key events in the organisation's history (up to 5):

Charitable status:
  Registration or reference no:

  If not a charity, describe status of the organisation:

  VAT registration no:

People involved
  numbers of full time staff: numbers of part time staff:
  numbers of volunteers: volunteer hours a year:
  individual membership: institutional membership:

Annual income
  total income:
  total raised from grants and donations:
  total self-generated:
  total expenditure:
  total assets:

continued overleaf

---

1. Organisation fact file continued

Mission statement:

Principal objects or purposes of the organisation:

Present policies and priorities:

Business plan last updated in:

Beneficial area or area over which the organisation operates:

Affiliations with other relevant organisations:

The organisation: what makes it unique or different and why its work is especially important (3 key facts):

Recent growth in the organisation and in the demand for its services (3 key statistics):

---

2. Credibility fact file

Last updated:

Successes

List your five greatest successes in the past five years:

Other recent successes and achievements of the organisation:

Main financial sponsors:

government and other official sources:

grant-making trusts:

business sponsors:

individual supporters:

prominent patrons and supporters:

Recent press or media coverage:

3. Credibility Box File

This is simply where you keep all the press coverage, statements, quotations, evaluations or other information about the organisation which endorse the value of its work. Once it's full, start pruning the out-of-date clippings.

4. A fundraising plan for the organisation

Fundraising always takes time, and it is sensible to plan well ahead. Ideally draw up a three or five-year budget of income and expenditure. The following is a suggestion for an income budget in order to plan your fundraising (an expenditure budget in this book would be so generalised as to be useless).

Start by looking at your income and expenditure over the last four or five years. Do you notice any trends (e.g. rise in salary or premises costs; fall in local authority grant; growth in income from grant-making trusts; increasing reliance on one source of income)? Make a note of them and make sure your fundraising plan takes full account of them. For example, if you have never had any company sponsorship, it will take time to build this up. Don't put £100,000 down in year one just because it looks good.

When compiling your figures, make a note of any assumptions and action points, particularly with regard to large chunks of income. Also, remember that this exercise is, at best, a guesstimate. You cannot guarantee future income, so if it appears you have got your projections wrong, change them.

Finally, be honest and realistic! The temptation is to write up income and write down expenditure, when it is more often the other way round.

Here are some possible budget headings you might use for your income projections.

Total budgeted or estimated expenditure for the year £ _____

Income to be raised (by category)

Investment income and bank interest	£ _____
Earned income from:	
contracts for service delivery	£ _____
other sale of services	£ _____
training & conferences	£ _____
publication sales	£ _____
other trading activities	£ _____
Legacies	£ _____
Grants from:	
central government	£ _____
local government	£ _____
other statutory sources	£ _____
trusts	£ _____
company donations	£ _____
business sponsorship	£ _____
other sources	£ _____
Public fundraising	
membership subscriptions	£ _____
fundraising events	£ _____
covenants/Gift Aid	£ _____

collections   £ _____

other   £ _____

Total income budgeted for the year   £ _____

Budgeted surplus or deficit   £ _____

Comments

Key dates:

Schedule of expiring grants

larger grants which are likely to be renewed (list sources/annual amount/expiry date/renewal action to be taken and by whom/comments)

larger grants which are unlikely to be renewed (list sources/annual amount/expiry date/suggestions for alternative sources of funding/comments)

Schedule of expiring contracts/service agreements:

major contracts/service agreements which are likely to be renewed

major contracts/service agreements which are unlikely to be renewed

Key fundraising events (timetable for who is doing what and by when)

covenant/Gift Aid tax reclaim (who does it by when)

131

5. Project fact file

This brings together information about the project you are raising money for

Last updated:

Description of the proposed project/purpose of the application (not more than 20 words):

The need for the project – three key facts:

Partner organisations (how and why are they involved):

Why it is so important to undertake the project at the present time (three key points):

The objectives of the project (three specific and measurable outcomes):

When will the above outcomes happen?

Methods which will be used to undertake the project:

Five key tasks you will undertake in the first year:

User involvement: how are the users or beneficiaries involved in the work?

Volunteer inputs: how are volunteers to be involved and what is the value of this?

How do you plan to disseminate any results or the outcome of the project?

How will the project will be evaluated?

Any consequences or anticipated future impact which will result from the project:

Estimated start date of the project:

Estimated completion date or term of the project:

Key people involved and relevant experience:

Outside advisers:

Any other details of the project which are particularly special or noteworthy:

6. Budget checklist – revenue project

Here is an outline budget for a revenue project. We have left space at the bottom for two subsequent revisions, the first in the light of your assessment of the fundraising potential of the project (you may wish to increase or reduce certain costs, or add to or subtract from the project), and the second to allow you to confirm or get better estimates for the major items of cost.

Project title

1st draft

	Year 1	Year 2	Year 3
Employment costs/salaries (inc. National Insurance)	....	....	....
Recruitment costs	....	....	....
Volunteer expenses/training costs	....	....	....
Project costs			
equipment	....	....	....
printing/stationery	....	....	....
post/telephone	....	....	....
travel/transport	....	....	....
training	....	....	....
evaluation	....	....	....
technical advice/consultancy	....	....	....
dissemination of results	....	....	....
other project costs	....	....	....
	....	....	....
	....	....	....
Overhead costs *			
office occupancy (rent/rates/heat/light etc.)	....	....	....
management & administration	....	....	....
central services (cleaning etc.)	....	....	....
depreciation	....	....	....
Other overhead costs	....	....	....
	....	....	....
	....	....	....
TOTAL	£...................	£...................	£...................

* State basis on which overhead costs have been apportioned to the project
State basis on which inflation has been allowed for in the second and third years
State any other relevant assumptions

	First revision			*Second revision*		
	Year 1	Year 2	Year 3	Year 1	Year 2	Year 3
TOTAL	....	....	....	....	....	....

7. Fundraising plan for the project

Just as you will need an income budget for the organisation, you will also need budgets for each of the projects that the organisation undertakes as part of its work. Having costed the project (see *6. Budget checklist*), you will need to draw up an income budget. You will need a separate column for each year of the project.

Firstly, categorise the budgeted income under the different heads:

- government and other statutory sources
- grant-making trusts and other charities
- business support (inc. sponsorship and gifts in kind)
- donations from members/individual supporters
- fundraising events and activities
- your organisation's own contribution
- other

Under each income source, you will need to list:

- total income to be raised from that source
- a list of grants raised or committed to date, and a total for this committed income
- a list of likely grants still being negotiated or decided, and a total for this probable income
- the total income still required
- any notes or comments

Compare your *Fundraising plan for the project* with 4. *A Fundraising plan for the organisation*. For example, are you aiming to raise the entire trusts budget for a single project? If so, (i) is this realistic, and
(ii) what about the other projects you are trying to raise money for?

You will need to keep your project plan up-to-date, recording grants when they come in and revising estimates and running totals accordingly. Where you fail to secure a major grant which you had been planning for, you may need to revise your whole approach. A contingency plan can alert you to the possibilities.

8. Keeping track of progress

You need to keep track of the progress of each key grant you have applied for. In the light of this, review the situation regularly and take action sooner rather than later. If you don't, you may end up with a large hole in your budget. For each grant, keep the following information:

Who you applied to

How much you asked for/expect

Name of person you sent it to

Who signed the letter

Date application was sent off

Expected decision date

Follow up action:

    (i) action already taken

    (ii) the possibilities of further action

    (iii) suggestions for possible alternative sources

Person responsible for negotiating the grant

9. Mobilising contacts

You can improve your chances significantly by developing good personal contacts with the trustees and others responsible for grants decisions in the bodies you are approaching. This section provides an 'audit' of the contacts that you, your colleagues, your trustees and your patrons already have as a start to mobilising their support. Remember too that your employee volunteers can be particularly important when approaching their employer.

For each of your colleagues, your trustees, your patrons, and possibly even some of your key supporters and most committed volunteers, keep a record of the following information.

Name:

Position/occupation:

Contact address/phone/fax/e-mail:

Any relevant skills they have and help they are prepared to give:

Useful contacts they are prepared to approach for support (or let you approach on their behalf):

    name/position/address/telephone of the contact

    funding body and their connection with it

    whether you or they will make the approach

    notes (e.g. what is the existing relationship with this contact/funding body)

The help you will want from your supporters will be anything from:

- Sounding the funder out
- Having a quiet, informal word over dinner
- Attending (or even making) a formal presentation of your project to the funder
- Signing a covering letter
- Asking formally for money face to face

Further reading

The following selection of useful publications are all available from the Directory of Social Change, 24 Stephenson Way, London NW1 2DP.

Forrester, S *The Arts Funding Guide 1997/98*, 4th edition, 1996, DSC

Smith, G *Asking Properly – The Art of Creative Fundraising*, White Lion Press Ltd, 1996 (this is particularly concerned with direct mailing to individuals)

Clarke, S and Norton, M *The Complete Fundraising Handbook*, 3rd edition, DSC, 1997

Lawrie, A *The Complete Guide to Business and Strategic Planning*, DSC, 1994

Lawrie, A *The Complete Guide to Creating and Managing New Projects*, DSC, 1996

Wells, C *The DIY Guide to Charity Newsletters*, DSC, 1995

Ali, M *The DIY Guide to Marketing*, DSC, 1996

Ali, M *The DIY Guide to Public Relations*, DSC, 1995

Smyth, J and Wallace, K *The Educational Grants Directory 1996/97*, 4th edition, DSC, 1996

Forrester, S; Mountfield, A and Patel, A *The Education Funding Guide*, DSC, 1995

The Environmental Funding Guide (available in 1998)

The Government Funding Guide (available in 1998)

Brown, P and Smyth, J *A Guide to Company Giving 1997/98*, 7th edition, DSC, 1997

Smyth, J and Wallace, K *A Guide to Grants for Individuals in Need 1996/97*, 5th edition, DSC, 1996

Holly, K *A Guide to Local Trusts in London*, DSC 1996

Casson, D *A Guide to Local Trusts in the Midlands*, DSC 1996

Casson, D *A Guide to Local Trusts in the North of England*, DSC 1996

Casson, D *A Guide to Local Trusts in the South of England*, DSC 1996

FitzHerbert, L; Forrester, S and Grau, J *A Guide to the Major Trusts Vol. 1 1997/98*, 6th edition, DSC, 1997

Brown, P and Smyth, J *A Guide to the Major Trusts Vol. 2 1997/98*, 3rd edition, DSC, 1997

Prabhudas, Y *Image-Building and Money-Raising for Hard-to-Sell Groups*, DSC, 1994

Brown, P; Casson, D and Smyth J *The Major Companies Guide 1996/97*, 4th edition, DSC, 1995

Lawrie, A *Managing Quality of Service*, DSC, 1995

FitzHerbert, L and Rhoades, L *The National Lottery Yearbook and Grant-seekers Guide 1997*, 2nd edition, DSC, 1997

Burt, E *Research and its Evaluation – A DIY Guide*, DSC, 1997

Prabhundas, Y *The Scottish Trusts Guide*, DSC, 1996

Eastwood, N and Smyth, J *The Sports Funding Guide*, DSC, 1995

Adirondack, S and Sinclair Taylor, J *The Voluntary Sector Legal Handbook*, DSC, 1996

Eastwood, N *The Youth Funding Guide*, DSC, 1997

The CD-ROM Trusts Guide, which includes *A Guide to the Major Trusts Vols. 1 and 2*, as well as the four *Local Trust Guides*, is also available from the DSC.

Note: from 1998, *The Major Companies Guide* and *A Guide to Company Giving* will be replaced by a single publication, *The Guide to UK Company Giving*.

The Plain English Campaign

The Plain English Campaign publishes books and runs courses with the aim of promoting clear, concise and effective use of written English. The following titles may be of use to anyone wanting to convey a powerful message in a simple but interesting way:

The A-Z of Alternative Words

Utter Drivel

How to Write Letters in Plain English

How to Write Reports in Plain English

A-Z Guide to Legal Words

Further details are available from The Plain English Campaign, PO Box 3, New Mills, High Peak SK22 4QP